Pastoral Authority
in Personal
Relationships

Pastoral Authority in Personal Relationships

SAMUEL SOUTHARD

Abingdon Press

Nashville and New York

PASTORAL AUTHORITY IN PERSONAL RELATIONSHIPS

Copyright © 1969 by Abingdon Press

Library of Congress Catalog Card Number: 69-12021

Scripture quotations unless otherwise noted are
from the Revised Standard Version of the Bible,
copyrighted 1946 and 1952 by the Division of
Christian Education, National Council of Churches,
and are used by permission.

The author wishes to express appreciation to *Pastoral Psychology* for portions of Chapters 5 and 7
which originally appeared in that periodical and
to *Religion in Life* for portions of Chapter 6 which
originally appeared in the summer, 1967 issue;
copyright © 1967 by Abingdon Press.

SET UP, PRINTED, AND BOUND BY THE
PARTHENON PRESS, AT NASHVILLE,
TENNESSEE, UNITED STATES OF AMERICA

Contents

Contents

1
The Problem of
Pastoral Authority

How can a person who has accepted a transcendent power over his own life enable others to accept and relate the power of God to their own lives? This central question of mission is especially focused in pastors, who represent spiritual authority. They are the transmitters of a sacred tradition, the teachers of the church, the representatives of God.

This is a weighty and often misused authority. It proved to be cumbersome in the post–World War II emphasis upon acceptance, nonjudgment, and ethical relativity. The minister who wished to be person-centered was the first to deny that he had authority.

But Christianity is an authoritative religion. Words like "submit," "obey," "surrender" are common in the Christian tradition. The basic text of faith and order, the Bible, contains direct commands for obedience.

First, the will of God is to be obeyed. So Peter proclaims, "We must obey God rather than men" (Acts 5:29). This will is known in Christ. To know him is to

7

obey him: "You call me Teacher and Lord; and you are right, for so I am" (John 13:13). The Christian disciple is a "captive" of Christ (II Cor. 10:5).

Second, the congregational and ecclesiastical leaders are to be obeyed. Members of the primitive church were told to esteem those who were "over" them (I Thess. 5:12), to obey the doctrine as taught by apostles (such as Paul; Rom. 16:17, 19). To "submit" to rulers of the flock was required (Heb. 13:17).

This is the counsel of authoritative religion, a system of power which through personal obedience would influence opinion, induce belief, lead to action. Those who submitted would be rewarded; those who rebelled would be punished.

The modern minister has inherited this role, and he cannot easily relieve himself of it. As a spiritual authority he is expected to be an evaluator of behavior, an upholder of standards, a mediator of godly acceptance or judgment.

This tradition is centered in personal relationships. As a survey in Chapter 4 will show, laymen expect ministers to be "spiritual guides." The most important part of the minister's work is expected to be his visitation of the sick and lonely, his counsel and understanding of Christian faith, his acceptance of persons through baptism and church membership, his counsel with those who are to be married, of those who are bereaved, and his directing of church lay workers.

The minister is resisted when he seeks to be an expert in social and political action, to give advice on work and career decisions, to be active in community relationships.

The clearest communication of this "spiritual authority" is to be found in a counseling relationship. When Dr. Robert Mitchell received questionnaires from 3,928 clergymen of eight denominations, he found that there was much less misunderstanding with laymen about "counselling parishioners on their personal problems" than there was about controversial topics in sermons or the administration of the congregation.[1]

It also seems that the *community* is willing to accept the minister as a guide in the area of personal problems. Whatever the reasons may be, people seek out a clergyman more often than any other professional person when they are in need of help with marriage, self-adjustment, or parent-child problems.[2]

It should be noted, however, that the clergyman is sought out as a *general* authority. People who cannot put their finger on the exact cause of their difficulty or who find that there is a defect in their relationship to another person are the ones who come first to a clergyman. On the other hand, if an individual has found that his difficulty is clearly within himself, then he first seeks out a physician.[3] The clergyman is consulted because he is the one who could recommend the "right" course of behavior rather than prescribe some change in personality organization.

[1] "Minister-Parishioner Relations" (Bureau of Applied Social Research, Columbia University, 1962), Sec. 9, p. 3.

[2] Gerald Gurin, *Americans View Their Mental Health* (New York: Basic Books, 1960), pp. 307-9.

[3] *Ibid.*, p. 312.

From these studies it sounds as though the minister is halfway between the stereotypes of policeman and psychiatrist. The clergyman is expected to have some definite "spiritual" principles which he can apply to the problems that people present to him. He is expected to know what is right and wrong, what will be accepted and what will be punished in this world or the world to come. But at the same time he has no power of enforcement in this life. Like the psychiatrist, he must depend upon the strength of his personal relationship to bring about changes in attitude and conduct.

The complexity of the problem is short-circuited by ministers who respond either as policemen or as psychiatrists. Some seek to enforce regulations, give final answers, manipulate the unwilling, and dominate the dependent. Others reject all judgment and adopt the popular stereotype of a counselor who hides all his opinions behind "reflective" attitudes. He may assure people that he is not "judgmental," but what does this do to his traditional role as an ethical teacher, educator, moral guide for the soul?

This book is addressed to the operational dilemma of a pastor's office and function. On the one hand, he represents and is committed to a transcendent Judge, Redeemer, Lord, who demands submission by all men. On the other hand, he must accept people as they are and refrain from imposing *his* judgments upon them. How can a representative of spiritual authority enable others to accept and relate the power of God to their own lives?

The Themes of Authority

An answer to the question of pastoral authority will involve at least three themes: discipleship, craftsmanship, and reconciliation.

Discipleship sets Christian authority in a special perspective. Jesus explained it this way:

You know that the rulers of the Gentiles lord it over them, and their great men exercise authority over them. It shall not be so among you; but whoever would be great among you must be your servant, and whoever would be first among you must be your slave; even as the Son of man came not to be served but to serve, and to give his life as a ransom for many. (Matthew 20:25-28.)

After examining these and other New Testament passages, the Roman Catholic theologian John L. McKenzie concluded: "The sayings reveal a new conception of society and of authority, which must be formed not on the model of secular government, but on the mission of Jesus himself." [4]

Christian authority is the continuation of the servant mission of the Lord. "Apostolic" authority is genuine when a witness is willing to suffer for the gospel. This is Paul's mark of authentic authority (II Cor. 11:23-28). An authoritative Christian is one who runs the risk of publicly witnessing in life and word to the grace which Christ has brought. All authority in Christian faith must take its meaning from Christ's ministry. He is the source

[4] *Authority in the Church* (New York: Sheed & Ward, 1966), pp. 31-32.

of power that legitimizes spiritual demands. Christians present him as the claim of God upon each life and the gift of God to every life. Judgment and forgiveness, law and grace are inseparable parts of the authoritative proclamation of a disciple.

Authority for a minister also implies craftsmanship. His power is the result of training as well as education. People respect pastoral opinions because the minister, like the doctor, is an "expert." The special proficiency of the minister is as a servant to men in spiritual need.

Craftsmanship assumes more authority when it is highly respected by the group to whom the expert is responsible. The group sets standards, which include instructions for the performance of a leadership task and often a period of supervision. In the case of the ministry, specialized training usually precedes ordination. Ordination in many denominations is a sign that a person has desirable spiritual, personal qualities and has fulfilled academic requirements.

Discipleship stresses the immediate authority of direct experience. Craftsmanship combines this with the mediated authority of a professional office. The goal of both kinds of authority is the reconciliation of man to God, of man to man. This is the unifying theme of the ministry. Pastoral authority is assumed for the sake of others. There is to be no worldly privilege for the minister, no special sacredness in his person. He is a man among men, but one who has been set apart to devote all time to reconciliation.

As Chapter 3 will illustrate, the American tradition understood reconciliation as evangelism. The clergyman was primarily a winner of souls. Great contempt was heaped upon "hireling clergy" who were more concerned for social status, salary, and ceremony than they were for revivals of "experimental" religion. The theme of reconciliation was, and may still remain, the dominant note of American pastoral authority.

The Professional Note

Immediate religious experience was the basis of American pastoral authority. "Heart religion" was much to be preferred over "head religion." The ministry was referred to as a "calling" rather than as a "profession."

But the growing membership, budget, and buildings of the nineteenth and twentieth centuries demanded craftsmanship as much as discipleship. In large organizations as many problems emerged in reconciling members to one another as in reconciling sinners to a Savior. The minister became a *church* authority, the leader of a prominent social institution. A professional note became prominent in the "call." A man must know what he was doing, get along with people, build up the organization, as well as save souls.

Because of his position in the established church organization, the minister must be authoritative in a variety of functions. Sociologically, these may be expressed as (1) the maintenance of traditional values, (2) sensitivity to personal feelings and community relationships, (3) power to move the church organization toward specific goals, and (4) influence over the lives of men that they and the world in which they live may be changed toward God.[5]

The authority of a minister will appear in prophetic and evangelistic forms when he is seeking to change men and movements; it will appear in pastoral emphasis when he is called upon to reflect feelings or understand group relationships; his authority as a priest or reminder of values comes through his preaching and sacramental ministry; organizational authority is manifested in his power to move the church toward a specific program of action.

Each of these aspects of authority is part of the other. The craftsmanship of the minister will be shown in his ability to keep all these manifestations of authority within the range of his responsible action and focus one or the other upon particular persons or conditions in an appropriate manner.

To meet these professional responsibilities, a minister can rely upon all the traditional designations of authority. These are (1) the derived authority that the minister has received from church and community tradition, (2) a legal responsibility to function as a representative of an established institution and to uphold the norms of that institution, (3) the charismatic hold which a saintly or heroic individual has upon those who hear him, and (4) the technical knowledge which a

[5] This is an adaptation by Hoyt Oliver of the field theories of Talcott Parsons. See Hoyt P. Oliver, "Professional Authority and the Protestant Ministry: A Stury of an Occupational Image" (Ph.D. dissertation, Yale University, 1967), and Talcott Parsons, "Pattern Variables Revisited," *American Sociological Review*, XXV (August, 1960), 467-83.

person offers without coercion to those who need his help.[6]

In the American religious system special emphasis is placed on charisma and helpful knowledge. One theologian, Daniel Day Williams, presents skill in personal encounter as the authentic power of a pastor. Although certain authority is conferred upon the minister and recognized by some who seek him, his "real personal authority arises out of the concrete incarnation of the spirit of loving service which by God's help becomes present in the care of souls." [7]

Authoritative Concern

How is concern to be conveyed within a system of authority? The first requirement is a minister's awareness of the ways others see him. Dr. Williams has described this in the contrast between the "public" and "hidden" exercise of the minister. For example, a person may acquiesce to what he conceives the authority to demand but remain passively resistant to what he thinks he is being told. The clergyman is publicly accepted but inwardly rejected. Also, there may be quite a difference between the actual thoughts of a minister and the way people expect him to think. A layman's experience with

[6] This last category, "Professional," was added by Talcott Parsons to the original list of Max Weber. See Talcott Parsons, *Essays in Sociological Theory* (rev. ed.; Glencoe, Ill.: The Free Press, 1954), pp. 34-49.

[7] Daniel Day Williams, *The Minister and the Care of Souls* (New York: Harper & Row, 1961), p. 43.

other authorities in the past can make a clergyman the target for many projected and outdated thoughts.

A second requirement is the minister's ability to see other people as they are. Without this insight there can be no dialogue, only intersecting monologues. To make the message of God personal, a counselor must know the person. A witness is not heard unless he has made contact with some vital area in the life of another. It is not enough to "faithfully proclaim the Word." The Word became flesh. Christian authority has been embedded in relationships, and our ability to understand others and project ourselves into their circumstances will give them the feeling that we look at problems with them. This can lead to the kind of pastoral judgment that Seward Hiltner has called "shared appraisal." [8] There is a decrease in defensiveness and a heightening of receptivity when an individual feels that a minister understands and enters into his concerns.

On the other hand, Christian counsel is more than empathetic creature-feeling. The authority of the minister is basically his ability to bring a transcendent power to bear upon our lives. The goal is holiness for a finite creature, rather than self-sufficient wholeness.

So the third requirement of authoritative concern is this: the ability of a minister to lead another to see himself as God sees him. To see God in this way is to know his concern for reconciliation. In God alone is the power of redemption. Thus a counselor fulfills the basic goal

[8] "Judgment and Appraisal in Pastoral Care," *Pastoral Psychology*, XVI (December, 1965), 43 ff.

of discipleship, to point men beyond the servant to the Master.

The concern of the Christian is for an authority beyond himself. As Peter T. Forsyth puts it, "Our only authority must be faith's object itself in some direct self-revelation of it." [9] The minister is a witness to that power beyond himself that can be revealed to any who will have faith. The faithfulness of the minister's witness will be checked by the tradition of the church, the written word of Scripture, and the personal experience of grace in an individual. Authority is therefore beyond both the minister and those whom he counsels. It is mediated through personal experience, but power is not in the experience itself. "Faith is a religious experience, but religious experience is not faith." [10] The unity that the minister seeks for himself and others is not functional wholeness, significant as this may be. His goal is a transcendent power that will direct him and others toward God.

Such statements sound very "spiritual" and are very satisfying to conservative-minded laymen who resist the minister's interest and involvement in psychology and social action.

I am not seeking to limit the interest of the minister; I am trying to increase the depth of his impact upon others. As Milton Rokeach has described authority in *The Open and Closed Mind*,[11] there are at least three

[9] *The Principle of Authority* (Naperville, Ill.: Alec R. Allenson, 1952), p. 20.
[10] *Ibid.*, p. 27.
[11] (New York: Basic Books, 1960.)

levels of personal penetration. On the periphery there are beliefs about the class struggle, changes in society, political and economic decisions. Beneath these are the "intermediate beliefs," authoritative decisions concerning God, human conduct, the state, and the family. Closest to the self-system are beliefs concerning personal identity and sureness about objects with which we come in contact on a daily basis. Here is where we decide if the world is friendly or unfriendly, if we are worthy or unworthy, if we are loved or unloved by a power beyond ourselves.

Especially in the last chapter of this book, we will be concerned about the penetration of authority to this deepest level of ideology. Although the rearrangement of political decisions and the changing of beliefs about human conduct or dogma can be significant, they do not have the depth or durability of a shift in personal loyalty or identity. This deeper reorientation has been called conversion. It may be brought about on a human level through anxieties within the individual or because of the boldness of one who witnesses to a new center of loyalty for the self.

The mission of the Christian is the transfer of authority. He speaks with authority about a power that others can make the center of their lives. The hearer of the word who becomes a "doer" will then be as much a disciple as any minister. The duty of the church is to proclaim "The kingdom is among you" by word and deed, so that men may faithfully say, "The kingdom is within me."

2
The Obedient
Servant

The certainty of Christian authority is an experienced faith in an engrafted word. The word is made known to us through personal experience, through the fellowship of believers, past and present, and through the written word, the Scriptures. The first of these, personal authority, has been briefly discussed in the previous chapter and will be a dominant theme in Chapters 5 and 6. These are the sections in which the face-to-face relationship of pastor and person is discussed. The personal meaning of authority will also be presented in the final chapter, on the ways in which a person is willing to accept authority. The authority of church and tradition will be presented in Chapters 3 and 4. The present chapter will consider the biblical basis for pastoral authority.

There is abundant biblical material on the source of authority, the model of authority, and our life of obedience to authority. There is not as much material on the organization and recognition of church authorities, but there are several references to the way in which authority is to be exercised within the Christian fellowship.

Free Obedience

The emphasis of modern biblical scholarship is upon Christian power in persons rather than in places, in attitudes rather than in offices. This emphasis begins in the question of sources for authority. To whom does a Christian owe obedience?

John Kennedy has presented four sources of authority for the Christian.[1] First, he is to obey what he knows of the will of God. So Peter proclaimed to the council of the Jews (Acts 5:29). Paul wrote the same to the Thessalonians (I Thess. 4:1). The first letter of John presents obedience to God's commandments as the assurance of our love for him (I John 5:2). Christ stated two obligations for every follower of his: the total love of God and the love of neighbor as self.

Second, Christ claimed obedience to his own lordship. This is the second source of Christian authority. This was astonishing to the people of his own day. They clearly perceived the note of authority in all that he said (Matt. 7:28-29). His claim to obedience was quite exclusive: "You have one master, the Christ" (Matt. 23:10). Those who surrendered to his exclusive claims were approved: "You call me Teacher and Lord; and you are right, for so I am" (John 13:13). This claim

[1] *Presbyterian Authority and Discipline* (Richmond, Va.: John Knox Press, 1965), pp. 68-71.

became the goal of the apostle Paul, that he might bring into captivity every thought to the obedience of Christ (II Cor. 10:5).

Third, the church and its leaders are sources of authority. In part this is obedience to sound teaching (Rom. 16:17, 19). One of the reasons for the exercise of authority was the danger that converts might stray away from sound teaching if they had company with those who would not obey the word (II Thess. 3:14). The Christian community was to watch over the souls of all those in his company and "give account" of the way in which each believer lived (Heb. 13:17). At times the command of obedience was very personal, as in Paul's admonition that the beloved Philippians follow his example or that a leader be followed because of his sacrificial work (II Cor. 7:15; Phil. 2:12; I Thess. 5:12-13).

Finally, there is the admonition for Christians to obey those who exercise lawful authority in the world. Children are to obey their parents, servants their masters, citizens the magistrates.

With all these authorities to obey, the Christian life might seem to be little more than compliance. But, as the Roman Catholic theologian John L. McKenzie has vigorously protested, obedience and submission are not ends in themselves. Authority is only one function of the Spirit, and it is given no specific place in the church or its offices.[2]

[2] *Authority in the Church*, pp. 65-66.

The obedience to which the Christian is called leads to freedom rather than to obsequiousness. The true servant of God lives without fear of the ordinances of men (Colossians 2). The opinion of the crowd about himself is a "small thing" in comparison with the judgment of Christ (I Corinthians 4). The servant of Christ is free from the terror of death, the bondage of sin, the enervating effects of guilt (Romans 6; Galatians 2–5). The disciple is even free to look at himself as he really is because he has submitted to "the perfect law . . . of liberty" (James 1:25). His acceptance before God as an adopted son gives him power to direct his imperfect life with insight and serenity.[3]

The New Authority

This radically free obedience must come from some spiritual source of which the world is not aware. The contrast between worldly and spiritual authority is presented in Matt. 20:25-28 (see p. 11). These words of Jesus reveal a new conception of both religion and authority, a model based upon the mission of Jesus himself rather than upon any order of society.

Jesus set the example in the menial service of washing the feet of his disciples (John 13:1-20). It is a new kind of service that he rendered. He is not the slave of men, but the obedient son of his Father in heaven. Because of

[3] For a discussion on "The Tension Between Authority and Freedom," see *ibid.*, pp. 162-74.

this obedience he is given power above all men. Miracles are a sign of his mission as the Son of the Father (John 5–7).

Jesus set severe limitations upon this great power. He would not use it to gain personal glory, to obtain quick results, or to satisfy his physical needs (Matthew 4). Also, he would not perform the traditional rabbinical service of arbiter in a dispute of two brothers over their inheritance (Luke 12:13-14). When there were disputes among his disciples concerning their status, he contrasted the greatness of a small child in his kingdom with the arrogance of rulers among the nations (Matt. 20:20-28). Self-assertion is specifically forbidden in the exercise of godly authority.

The climax of the new servanthood was the voluntary surrender of the Messiah to the authorities of this world. When the time had come, he left the garden for Golgotha. It was because of this perfect and sacrificial obedience that the disciples saw him highly exalted (Philippians 2).

Personal Responsibility

The coming of Jesus made authority personal. He became the model; his life was the example; there was no office or place to substitute for the true credentials of sacrificial service.

The only special position is given to Simon Peter. In explaining the reference to Peter as a "rock" in Matt. 16:13-20, John McKenzie states:

Peter, who by the revelation of the Father has had an insight into the Messiahship of Jesus, exhibits the kind of faith on which the group can rest securely. The rock upon which the Church rests is the faith of Peter not understood as a merely personal act, but as embodying the faith upon which the Church depends for the fulfillment of her mission.[4]

The duty of Peter and any other apostle is the fulfillment of mission, whether it be proclamation, witness, or baptizing. There is nothing absolute about the leadership of Peter or of any other apostle. It is responsibility accepted and met. It is service in action.[5]

In the fulfillment of this mission the mark of an apostle is not his status in the world or the church but his patient suffering on behalf of Christ. As was said earlier, these are the marks of a genuine apostle, according to Paul (see also I Cor. 4:4-13; Gal. 6:17).

What are some of the personal implications of this kind of commission? First, the New Testament writers assume that affliction could be the lot of any aggressive Christian (I Thess. 3:1-4). Second, the apostle Paul admitted that persecution could crush him personally (II Cor. 1:8). Third, suffering was not discussed unless it had some specific purpose for the good of others (I Cor. 4:8-14). Fourth, an apostle who suffered for the sake of Christ was not bitter (Phil. 1:12-18). Fifth, there was no rejoicing in persecution except for the sake of the church (Col. 1:24-29). Sixth, the result of suffering

[4] *Ibid.*, p. 42.
[5] For a discussion of the functions of the apostolic office, see *ibid.*, p. 51.

was not to exalt a person but to make him more humble (II Cor. 11:30).

Suffering, like obedience, is not an end in itself. It is a part of discipleship that may be required of pioneers in the faith.

That which is the responsibility of the leader is also the responsibility of each member of the congregation. Members of the body of Christ are to admonish one another (Rom. 15:14; I Cor. 3:16; II Thess. 3:14-15), to have a care for one another; for if one member suffers, all the members suffer (I Cor. 12:26).

This mutual responsibility has traditionally been described as the "priesthood of believers," but the meaning is ambiguous. John Calvin thought that it did away with the need for any mediation between the individual believer and Christ, the high priest. To Zwingli it meant that each Christian would dedicate himself wholly to God. To Luther it meant that each member was responsible for prayer and action on behalf of every other member.[6]

Whichever interpretation a person prefers, he will find that the power of the priesthood is in Christ alone. The ministry of one member to another is authentic when it "[builds] up the body of Christ" (Eph. 4:12).

The essential authority of Christian ministry is life and service. We identify a disciple by the quality of life that Jesus portrayed with his people. Paul sums up the meaning of a disciple's authority when he speaks of the

[6] For a summary see T. W. Manson, *Ministry and Priesthood: Christ's and Ours* (Richmond, Va.: John Knox Press, 1959), p. 37.

"demonstration of the Spirit and power" (I Cor. 2:4).
Here is the personal appeal that grips the life of another
person.[7]

Pastoral Ministries

With so much emphasis upon the priesthood of the
laity and the servanthood of the congregation, students
of ecclesiology may wonder what has happened to the
great debates of the last generation about apostolic succession, the orders of the ministry, the distinctions between bishop, priest, and people.

A résumé of this debate is given by Anthony T. Han-
son in his introduction to *The Pioneer Ministry*.[8] Han-
son's conclusion is that most of the questions raised in
debates about the ministry cannot be proved decisively
from history or Scripture. He therefore turns from the
question of ministerial succession to the relation of the
ministry to the church. He concludes that ministers as a
separated group of servants have specific tasks beyond
that assigned to all members. First and foremost, they
are to preach the gospel. This is to be done by their lives
as well as by their words. Whether in deed or in word,
the minister is to be a pioneer of the faith. His purpose
is to be a representative man of God before the world.

The task of the ordained ministry is to serve the
church in order that every member may be an apostle

[7] For an exposition of these and related passages, see R. R. Williams,
ed., *Authority and the Church* (Naperville, Ill.: Alec R. Allenson,
1965), pp. 44 ff.

[8] (Philadelphia: The Westminster Press, 1961), pp. 85 ff.

who serves the world (I Cor. 3:18; 4:16). In this way the usual pattern of church-ministry-world is reversed to be ministry-church-world.[9] The relationship of the minister to individual members of the congregation is therefore of crucial importance. Through the minister each member can receive guidance and strength for apostolic life and service. Members do not sustain the minister so that he can represent them in the world; they set him apart to provide special guidance for *their* ministry in church and community.

The current emphasis of biblical theology is clearly upon functional authority rather than constituted authority. In his study of Luke-Acts, Thomas Wieser writes, "Authority for Luke resides in the act of witnessing which depends on the authentication by the Kyrios who is present in the Spirit." [10] He continues, "The authority for such witness does not rest in the association with Jesus in the past. Peter does not actually recite his experience in Caesarea. He refers to what God has done, 'giving the Spirit to them' (15:8). Peter's authority ultimately consists in pointing to this divine act." [11]

Corporate Discipline

The New Testament emphasis is upon a ministering church with certain gifted individuals, called by the

[9] *Ibid.*, p. 65.
[10] Thomas Wieser, ed., *Planning for Mission* (New York: World Council of Churches, 1966), p. 28.
[11] *Ibid.*, p. 29.

Holy Spirit through the church to preach, teach, and live the sacrifice of Christ to the congregation and, through the congregation, to the world. A minister might pioneer in the literal sense of establishing faithful colonies throughout the world, but this would not be the end of his mission. His "pioneering" spirit is essentially interpersonal; he seeks to challenge and build up converts to continue the apostolic mission themselves.

A congregation in mission must be a disciplined body of believers. In the New Testament this is described both as discipleship and as admonition and correction. Discipleship demanded discipline because it involved radical decision. Günther Bornkamm, Dietrich Bonhoeffer, and others have described discipleship as the determination to abandon everything to follow Christ.[12]

The disciple who has accepted God's judgment upon his own life passes on this judgment to others in the awareness of his own sinfulness. In his study of discipleship in Matthew, Martin Franzmann writes: "The disciple's characteristic act is that of the repentant man calling his fellow sinner to repentance, and the accent is on forgiveness. The goal of the disciple's activity is the removal of the speck from his brother's eye—after he has removed the log from his own." [13] The authority of a surrendered life leads to a shared appraisal of the need of others for one Lord.

[12] Günther Bornkamm, *Jesus of Nazareth*, tr. Irene and Fraser McLuskey (New York: Harper & Row, 1960), p. 146; Dietrich Bonhoeffer, *The Cost of Discipleship*, tr. R. H. Fuller (2nd rev. ed.; New York: The Macmillan Company, 1960), p. 7.

[13] *Follow Me* (St. Louis: Concordia Publishing House, 1961), p. 60.

The demand for responsible commitment was given in a number of New Testament verbs: "instruct," "admonish," "warn," all of them from one Greek root, *nouthesia* (Rom. 15:14; I Cor. 4:14; I Cor. 10:11; Eph. 6:4; Col. 3:16; II Thess. 3:15).

If there was a need for individual correction, the church was first to express this through an individual, then through a group, and finally by corporate action (I Cor. 5:1-13). The progression of power demonstrates the limitation of individual authority. One Christian may be a witness to another, but only a congregation of believers can act in discipline toward another.

Although Peter spoke direct condemnation of Ananias and Sapphira (Acts 5:1-4) and Paul warned against the sins of individuals (e.g. I Cor. 5:5), the proceedings for discipline were clearly to be carried out by a group. No ordained or unordained member of the congregation pronounced judgment by himself. The development of this understanding of corporate authority and discipline in the American church will be explored in the following chapter.

Definitions of Authority

To summarize biblical statements on authority, we may speak of Christian authority as the power to influence opinion, induce belief, and so lead to action in areas defined as spiritual by a group of persons who acknowledge Christ as Lord. The power is considered legitimate when it conveys the spirit of Christ to others. It is to be exercised in the spirit of humble service which

Jesus exemplified with his disciples. It is binding upon those who volunteer acceptance of the life of Christ as their model.

Pastoral authority is presented more as a function than as an office in the New Testament. It is the expression of personal concern for others, either to sustain or to restrain, to console or to discipline. Its object is the shared appraisal of strengths and weaknesses which may be redirected toward wholeness or holiness.

Pastoral authority is a shared responsibility in the narratives of the early church. Believers are priests to one another. All are ministers, but some have special functions in teaching and preaching that lead to their ordination. The minister prepares the church to minister to the world.

From these definitions we may begin to formulate some answers to the basic question: How can a person who has accepted a transcendent power over his own life and who represents this spiritual authority enable others to accept and relate the power of God to their own lives? The first and essential answer is that authority is appealing when it comes through a broken heart. The minister who has humbled himself before God, who has surrendered his life to obedient service, is authentic when he talks about the same process before another person. His spirit speaks for his words. This is the first meaning of "spiritual." It is the attitude of humble and grateful servants before their heavenly Father.

The second meaning of spiritual centers upon Christ. It is an interest in his life and message. At times it is expressed in an eagerness to hear all a person would say about love and hate, guilt and forgiveness, the mission and meaning of life and death. These are the subjects that count in a spiritual scale of values. At other times we identify our own allegiance to Christ by saying what these values mean to us in the light of our understanding of our Lord's teaching. This is personal, yet objective, witness. It is a sign that we know what we are talking about, just as we show by our attitudes what we feel about God. So the minister's authority grows subjectively and objectively, silently and verbally. He shows by his life and proclaims by his words the reality of God's reign in a representative man.

3
The American Exhorter

The ministry represents God to man and man to God. Discipleship and craftsmanship are combined, for the minister must not only lead a life of obedience to God, but also use personal skill in leading others to reconciliation with God. A divine call authenticates his witness; professional knowledge enables others to hear and respond to what he professes.

The ministry also represents the ways in which an age and a region respond to God. The more a minister reflects the concerns of his society, the easier will be his access to people, but the greater will be the danger that his presentation of God will be obscured by accommodation to a culture.

The uneasy balance between the authority of God and man can be demonstrated in the development of American Protestantism. It is a movement that grew strong with an emphasis upon personal profession of faith and freedom from established religion. The most
32

representative characteristic was revivalism.[1] This set the power of spirituality in the mold of an evangelistic ministry.

But the very exuberance of personal religious experience altered the message toward its most popular appeal. This was the primitive, provincial, anti-intellectual character of frontier America. As evangelical Protestantism took on these characteristics, the authority of the ministry was channeled through personal piety, biblical authority, and religious experience.

Primitivism and Provincialism

In rebellion against established authority in church and state, post-Revolutionary War evangelists were sure that they spoke for *original* authority. This was "New Testament Christianity." Most of Christian history after the first century was "Popery." With little appreciation for the past in a country looking to the future, revivalists concentrated on change in the present. "You can change your hearts now!" was the exhortation of Charles Finney.

The authority for this announcement was "primitive Christianity," the model was the Pentecostal message of Peter (Acts 2), the rationale was the writings of the apostle Paul. The American church was to be the reincarnation of apostolic preaching, fellowship, and organization.

This appeal of the primitive proliferated on the

---

[1] Perry Miller, *The Life of the Mind in America* (New York: Harcourt, Brace & World, 1965), pp. 7 ff.

American frontier. The most successful exponent of a restoration of the "ancient order of things" was Alexander Campbell. For Campbell, authority was absolute. It must be without error. The only infallible source that Campbell would accept was the Bible.[2]

The authority of church and ministry was, therefore, the authority of the Scripture. That which was allowed in the Scripture was to be allowed in the church and ministry, and that which was not spoken of in the Scripture was not to be allowed in any church of Christ.

Alexander Campbell came to this position even before he began to preach. In 1810 the Pittsburgh Synod rejected his father's request for membership in that Presbyterian body. They noted among other things that the father had encouraged the preaching of the son without proper authority. In answering the synod several days later, Alexander stated that the Scripture knows no difference between clergy and laity, so their objection was invalid and his preaching would open the door for all laymen to preach.[3]

There were other men on the old southwestern frontier who felt the same way. When five Kentucky Presbyterian ministers were suspended in 1803, they did not repent of their views that "the sinner has power to believe in Christ at any time." Instead, Marshall, Stone, McNemar, Dunlavy, and Thompson replied that no revocation of ecclesiastical privilege could annul "the

[2] *The Christian Baptist,* revised by D. S. Burnet from the 2nd ed. (H. S. Bosworth, 1858), Vol. I, p. 12; Vol. 2, p. 79.
[3] Robert Richardson, *Memoirs of Alexander Campbell* (Philadelphia: J. B. Lippincott & Co., 1868), I, 346.

original call of God, nor the obligation of the candidate
to obey. These principles are confirmed, both by the
New Testament and church history." [4]

The dominant religious characteristic of the nineteenth century was described by Richard Hofstadter in
this way: "The objective was to return to the pure
conditions of primitive Christianity, to which Scripture
alone would give the key. Even those who disliked this
tendency in American religion could see how central
it was." [5]

This type of biblical authority combined several psychological and sociological characteristics: individualism and infallibility, immediacy and literalism, illiteracy
and anti-intellectualism.

Individualism and biblical infallibility grew up together on the frontier. Self-reliant and often self-taught
men would acknowledge no intermediary for an understanding of the Bible. Elder William Kinkade explained
his "Bible doctrine" in terms of this background:

I was raised on the frontiers of Kentucky, in the midst of
the Indian war, where men were only respected in proportion
to their valor and skill in fighting Indians and killing wild
beasts. . . .

When I got religion I had but little learning; I could bare-
ly read and write, and that but very indifferently. . . . I laid
aside my leather hunting-shirt, my rifle-gun, and butcher-

[4] John Rogers, *The Biography of Elder Barton Warren Stone,
Written by Himself: With Additions and Reflections* (Cincinnati: J. A.
& U. P. James, 1847), p. 182.

[5] Richard Hofstadter, *Anti-Intellectualism in American Life* (New
York: Alfred A. Knopf, 1963), p. 83.

knife, and left my father's house and my beloved woods to travel and preach the Gospel. But before I started to preach, I thought it was necessary to buy a Bible, and as I had no money, I agreed to work for a Presbyterian man for one. He let me have it for five days' work, and although I had to grub bushes in a briar patch, I think it was the best bargain I ever made; I have it yet. It is a little pocket Bible without note, comment, or marginal reference. By reading it I formed my present views of religion . . . without the assistance of commentators, and before I had seen a concordance, nor had I at that time ever read a word from the pen of a Unitarian.

Although I have been a scholar in several schools . . . I [am] thankful to God that the independence of mind which grew up with me in my native woods has never forsaken me. I have at all times dared to oppose any thing that I did not think was right.[6]

All creeds, confessions, and theological opinions were to be tested in the light of personal feelings about God. If some part of a theological system did not fit a man's experience, he might reject that doctrine. So Barton Warren Stone and others gave up certain Calvinistic beliefs, such as total depravity.[7] Stone also rejected the language of the creed, "Eternally begotten," because he could not find the phrase in the Bible.[8]

John Smith had been trying to understand the subject of divine election and had preached it several times, including the Calvinistic interpretation of infant dam-

[6] Levi Purviance, *The Biography of Elder David Purviance* (Dayton: B. F. and G. W. Ells, 1848), pp. 204-5.

[7] William G. West, *Barton Warren Stone* (Nashville: The Disciples of Christ Historical Society, 1954), p. 94.

[8] *Ibid.*, pp. 84-85.

nation. But, when his two older children died in a fiery cabin, he argued, "My children are happy, for they were innocent," and put aside the doctrine of infant damnation.[9]

In time, individualism and infallibility became weapons of anti-intellectualism. The *Journal* of the General Conference of the Methodist Episcopal Church South for 1906 included a statement from the bishops that those who look to the pulpit for spiritual guidance want the authoritative statement of infallible truth and not the methods of critical research or the varied phases of theological inquiry. In the South and West, illiteracy reinforced anti-intellectualism. When an early Georgia Baptist leader, Jesse Mercer, sought in one sermon on the wisdom and power of God to describe the motions of the earth upon its axis and its annual motions around the sun, he was questioned by the people. They told him that Joshua had commanded the sun to stand still; therefore, the sun must go around the earth.[10]

Evangelism protected the unlearned who were pious against loss of self-esteem. The most famous evangelist of the 1830's, Charles Finney, probably with much justification, proclaimed it a *"solemn fact . . .* that the great mass of young ministers who are educated accomplished very little" (in revivalism). He felt that "plain men . . . acquainted with human nature, are ten times

[9] John A. Williams, *Reminiscences* (Cincinnati: F. L. Rowe, 1898), pp. 90-93, 110.
[10] Charles Galloway, "Thomas Griffin," *The Methodist Review* (Methodist Episcopal Church South), LII (July, 1903), 533.

better qualified to win souls than those who are educated on the present principle." [11] Abel Stevens pleaded in the 1850's for a return to "earnest simplicity and directness." He decried the "shams" of "dogmatic theology" and urged "experimental religions upon all people." [12]

Whether a person was illiterate or not, he might easily fall under the spell of a direct evangelistic appeal. The immediacy of the evangelist's message went with the literalism of his biblical authority. In an unlettered, unpretentious society, men were content to see selected verses "plainly," find confirmation for them in personal experience, and believe.

Literalism was especially appealing to those who wished to uphold the social status quo. Biblical passages on slavery were used in the South to justify the white man's responsibility for holding the inferior Negro in bondage.[13] A Charleston, South Carolina, Lutheran minister declared:

The teachings of the Bible are the most effective weapons that are used. . . . Our representatives in Congress used the argument contained in the Scriptures, and their opponents

[11] Charles Finney, *Lectures on Revivals of Religion* (New York: Fleming H. Revell Co., 1898), pp. 178-80.

[12] *Essays on the Preaching Required by the Times* (New York: Carlton & Phillips, 1856), pp. 18-24.

[13] "The Moral Philosophy of Slavery" in William Sumner Jenkins, *Pro-Slavery Thought in the Old South* (Gloucester, Mass.: Peter Smith, 1959). Walter Posey, "The Slavery Question in the Presbyterian Church in the Old Southwest," *Journal of Southern History*, XV (August, 1949), 311-24.

dared not tell them that the historical parts (and all that refers to slavery is historical) were uninspired and untrue.[14]

The above quotation demonstrates the provincialism of American pastoral authority. This, along with primitivism, was especially strong in the South and West. The minister had to appeal to the lay audience for support. He might have the authority of the Bible on his side, but he needed a voluntary congregation to support his principles. Leonard Bacon wrote from New Haven in May, 1852, that "parochial and self-governed churches . . . is the distinctively American method of religious organization." [15] "Local autonomy" dominated. Although this led to some disgraceful compromises on social issues in the nineteenth and twentieth centuries, the "voluntarism" of American churches produced two powerful sources of authority. One was the involvement of laymen in all phases of the church's life. The minister depended upon laymen not only for financial support but also for administration, teaching, and much of the evangelizing and pastoral care that had been traditionally expected of the clergy alone.

The second benefit was to increase the spiritual impact of the minister's authority. An observer of the 1850's commented that in America even a bishop "maintains his authority for the most part only by his personal character and judicious counsel." [16]

[14] Jenkins, *Pro-Slavery Thought in the Old South*, p. 207.

[15] Cited in Sidney E. Mead, "The Rise of the Evangelical Conception of the Ministry in America," in H. R. Niebuhr and D. D. Williams, eds., *The Ministry in Historical Perspectives* (New York: Harper & Row, 1956), p. 212.

[16] *Ibid.*, p. 214.

Calling and Anticlericalism

Personal character was one source of respect for the clergy, but it must be combined with a "call to preach." Common to character and call was the experience of conversion. George Gillespie wrote in 1742, "The causes of . . . decay among many others I conceive to be . . . our admission of young men to the ministry without examination of them in soul experiences and a strict search into their actions, if holy and exemplary." [17] In the middle colonies there was a bitter fight over insistence upon an examination of the spiritual experiences of a candidate for the ministry, the proclamation of his call, and the emphasis upon conversion and regeneration.[18] There was no resistance to the charismatic quality of a call among Baptists, Methodists, and Disciples. These, with the "new side" Presbyterians, emphasized conversion, calling, and character. The more conservatively minded "old side" Presbyterians emphasized personal piety and the knowledge of God, all in conformity to the authoritative judgment of the Bible.[19]

Personal experience and conversion were backgrounds for a "call to preach." Sometimes the experience was quite vivid. John Smith grew up in a section of frontier

[17] Cited in Elwyn Smith, *The Presbyterian Ministry in American Culture* (Philadelphia: The Westminster Press, 1962), p. 34.

[18] For a summary of the controversy see *ibid.*, Chapter 3, and for a more extensive discussion see L. J. Trinterud, *The Forming of an American Tradition* (Philadelphia: The Westminster Press, 1949).

[19] Smith, *The Presbyterian Ministry in American Culture*, pp. 143-58.

Appalachia where a vision or a voice was a sign of God's call. Although Smith had thought for some time that he should be a minister, he felt that he was too unimaginative to see a "ghostly vision." Therefore, he prayed to God for some simple sign. It came in the form of a dangerous ox that almost gored him. Holding the horns of the bellowing animal, Smith declared, "If the Lord should be with me in this extremity, and deliver me out of this trouble, I will know assuredly that he wants me to preach, and I will no longer scruple to be ordained." [20]

If a man did not have some feeling of "calling," he would feel incomplete. Barton Warren Stone was encouraged by one of his professors to enter the ministry. Stone said that he had no assurance of being divinely called and sent, but that if he were encouraged to do this work, he would begin it.[21]

This charismatic authority was considered superior to any other. When Joseph Thomas, about twenty years old, was asked by a Presbyterian minister for his license to preach, Thomas replied that he had a command to preach the gospel. When asked about his master, he said that he had one master, Christ. When asked for credentials, he produced the Bible and said it was signed with the blood of the great head of the church, Christ. Thomas then asked the minister about his relation to Christ, and when satisfied they had "great

[20] John A. Williams, *Life of Elder John Smith* (Cincinnati: The Standard Publishing Company, 1904), p. 63.

[21] Rogers, *The Biography of Elder Barton Warren Stone*, p. 12.

happiness in conversing about the things of God." [22]

The emphasis upon conversion and calling led to a particular type of anticlericalism. There was no widespread movement against all clergy and churches, but there was a concentrated attack upon educated and established clergy. Primitivists such as Alexander Campbell or Walter Scott led in these attacks. Walter Scott exclaimed, "Dear Lord, when I reflect that I have spent twenty years of my life under the noisy verbosity of a Presbyterian clergyman, without receiving the least degree of light from the Holy Word of God. . . ." [23] Alexander Campbell denounced the arrogant claims of the clergy to christen infants, confirm, celebrate matrimonial rites, attend the corpse to the grave, consecrate the ground, interpret the Scriptures.[24] In his opinion "the clergy have ever been the greatest tyrants in every state, and at present they are, in every country in Europe, on the side of the oppressors of the people who trample on the rights of men." [25] *The Christian Baptist* contained numerous satires against the richness of the clergy and of churches, especially in England.

A Baptist joined with the "restorationists" in resisting the authority of education and social position for clergymen. The clerk of the Kehukee Baptist Association in Virginia noted in 1803 that Baptists arose in New England because they opposed the Presbyterian churches

[22] Joseph Thomas, *The Life of the Pilgrim, Joseph Thomas* (Winchester, Va.: J. Foster, 1817).

[23] *The Christian Baptist*, Vol. I, No. 5 (December, 1823).

[24] *The Christian Baptist*, Vol. I, No. 3 (October 6, 1823).

[25] *The Christian Baptist*, Vol. II, No. 6 (January 3, 1825).

which "would admit none to the ministry, only men of classical education, and many of their ministers apparently seemed to be unconverted." In contrast, he thought that the Baptist ministers were "exceeding pious and zealous men, and their labors wonderfully blessed." [26]

Baptists in the South were content with the authority of character and calling for one hundred fifty years. A Southern Baptist Committee on Theological Education estimated in 1949 that one third of the ministers "never went beyond high school." [27]

Methodists exhibited little anticlericalism and gradually permitted the education of more and more of their ministers to influence theology and ecclesiology. But they were certainly one with the Disciples and Baptists in emphasizing the minister's calling, and most especially his calling to preach. H. S. Thrall of Texas wrote in 1857:

The candidate having been obligated and inducted into the ministry, what is his first duty? To make pastoral visits to the sick? to superintend Sunday-schools? to teach? to collect money for benevolent purposes? All these things he might have done as a layman, and may still attend to, as circumstances may permit; but he now has a duty paramount to all these. The first great duty of a minister of the gospel is, *to preach!*—TO PREACH! As ye go, PREACH! [28]

[26] Joseph Biggs, *Minutes of the Kehukee Baptist Association, 1803* (Historical Collection of the Southern Baptist Convention), pp. 34-35.
[27] *Southern Baptist Convention Book of Reports, 1949*, p. 310.
[28] "Methodist Preachers and Preaching," *Quarterly Review of the Methodist Episcopal Church South*, XI (October, 1857), 607.

In 1895 a south Georgia Methodist wrote in the same magazine: "God's chosen plan of saving sinners is by preaching." [29]

The primary object of preaching was the conversion of sinners. The evangelist described the joy of Christian experience, his feelings about conversion. Instead of preparing a sermon that described the way to heaven, the exhorter walked along the way and told the audience how he felt about it. In an 1808 sermon to Methodists in Baltimore, William McKendree described the "blessed effects upon the heart of the healing of God." He rejoiced at "spiritual deliverance from the bondage of sin." Nathan Bangs recorded: "Such was the confidence inspired in his wisdom and integrity, in his zeal and prudence in promoting the cause of God, and such a halo of glory seemed to surround his character, that the finger of Providence appeared to point to him." [30] The congregation began to shout, sob, and groan. One large, athletic-looking preacher, sitting by editor Bangs, suddenly fell from his seat as if pierced by a bullet, and even the editor was stirred by the experience. Exhortation was, as Abel Stevens called it, the "general habit" of nineteenth-century Methodism.[31]

If this kind of preaching produced decisions for Christ and the church, then the minister and the au-

[29] *Ibid.*, XLI (May-June, 1895), 232.

[30] Nathan Bangs, *History of the Methodist Episcopal Church* (New York: Carlton & Phillips, 1853), II, 238.

[31] *Essays on the Preaching Required by the Times*, p. 128.

dience concluded that he had authority from God to proclaim his message.

In summary, the majority of American Protestants in the nineteenth century would accept a minister as authoritative if he communicated his conversion and sense of divine calling through pious character and fervent preaching. Conversions either through personal conversation or revivalism were sure signs of his power from God.

Caring and Supervision

This popular stereotype of ministerial authority was magnified by preachers who held "big meetings." A contrast was sometimes made between the evangelist and the settled pastors who acted as bishops of their flock. In describing these two classifications, John Williams wrote in 1898 that the bishops "visited and cheered the sick, saw that the poor around us were not neglected, and consoled with soothing words the bereaved who wept at the coffins of their lost ones." [32]

This distinction is useful when we think of the authority of the minister in personal relationships. Most of the men who held "big meetings" in the nineteenth century were too often traveling and speaking for personal contacts with individuals. They set a pattern, while others ministered to the people.

Personal contacts were sometimes described by the "located" clergymen who held pastorates in the cities and county seats of nineteenth-century America. Ben-

[32] Williams, *Reminiscences*, p. 219.

jamin Palmer describes some of his pastoral calls on behalf of the First Presbyterian Church in New Orleans. One was with a gentleman who speculated in whiskey and was so often away from home and drunk that he feared for his marriage. Palmer told him to get out of the liquor business, return home, and resume the law practice he had abandoned. The pastor also described numerous visits with a person suffering from yellow fever and other diseases. His usual approach was to speak to the people of their faith in Christ and to urge conversion.[33]

In the more settled cities of the eastern seaboard an authoritative pastoral ministry could be seen in such men as Ichabod Spencer, who wrote down many of his conversations with people in *A Pastor's Sketches.* Whether the conversation was with a visiting evangelist, a Methodist itinerant, or an established Presbyterian pastor, there was an appeal to personal experience and the guidance of the Scriptures.

Along with the individual conversations, there were opportunities for care and supervision through "class meetings." These were weekly meetings of eight or more Methodists who met for prayer, exhortation, mutual protection, and "seeking the power of Godliness." A layman was appointed class leader. Either he or a visiting "circuit rider" would lead in prayer and exhor-

---

[33] P. C. Johnson, *The Life and Letters of Benjamin Morgan Palmer* (Richmond, Va.: Presbyterian Committee of Publication, 1906), pp. 183-88, 298-99. Thirteen articles of Palmer, "From the Pastor's Portfolio," were printed in the *Southwestern Presbyterian*, beginning in April, 1869.

tation and urge others to join them. Sometimes the leader or minister would then walk from person to person and hear if he were "orderly or disorderly" in his life. In some societies the rest of the members sang while one was being interrogated.

To uphold the purity of the church and to keep weak persons from straying, a class leader or circuit rider might "regulate" a man who whipped his wife or told stories about other people. That is, the person might be excluded from communion or dropped from the church rolls. On a circuit the minister might make his own decision about discipline. In more settled communities the decision was made by the church and conference.

Baptists and Presbyterians had no small group meetings for edification, but they joined with the Methodists in using discipline as a means of watchfulness and supervision. They felt it was the responsibility of the church to shepherd the pilgrims safely through the world. The lay leaders of Presbyterian churches, the elders, were responsible with the minister for the care and supervision of members. Among the Baptists a committee might be appointed to call upon an erring member, and a final decision would then be made by the entire congregation.[34]

The authority of the congregation over the life of individual members did not survive the upward change of social circumstances in major denominations. Among

[34] See Liston O. Mills, "The Relationship of Discipline to Pastoral Care in Frontier Churches, 1800-1850: A Preliminary Study," *Pastoral Psychology*, XVI (December, 1965), 22-34.

Congregationalists, Emil Oberholzer has traced the decline of church discipline to the decade following the Great Awakening. The Revolutionary War and the impact of the Enlightenment disrupted the old religious tradition of New England and the middle colonies.[35]

In the South and West the rise in social status defeated the church's concern. Professor W. J. Sasnett of Emory College, Georgia, wrote in 1851 that many of those "whose position in society secures to them a leading influence, are adverse to the humbling spiritual exercises appropriate to class meetings, and it is under the blighting spell of their indifference, if not actual opposition, that the Church in many quarters regard them with unconcern." [36]

All that remained of religious authority over personal life was the exhortation of the evangelist and the personal character of the pastor. A tradition of biblical authority, ministerial "spirituality," and personal religious experience had been established. Their influence is still to be seen in the modern concepts of pastoral authority which will be presented in the following chapter.

[35] Emil Oberholzer, *Delinquent Saints* (New York: Columbia University Press, 1956), pp. 239 ff.

[36] *Quarterly Review of the Methodist Episcopal Church South*, V (April, 1851), 282.

4
Twentieth-century
Authority

American Protestants have been more concerned about
persons of authority than places of authority. The emphasis has been upon function rather than upon status.
This has been a reflection of the evangelical interest in
individual salvation, personal piety, and lay responsibility. The conversion of souls was the chief aim of the
ministry, and authority was granted to evangelists as the
chief inquirers of religion in man.

The power of spiritual persuasion was paramount.
Any discipline of individuals was handled by a church
court rather than by the pastor alone or in concert with
secular authorities. The parishioner who was the subject
of this care and supervision could accept or reject the
church's decision according to his own acceptance or
rejection of its authority.

Church discipline ceased to be a significant force in
American Protestantism before the Civil War. If the
specific authority of a church over the life of individuals has not been accepted for over a hundred

49

years, what can we say about the authority of the minister who represents the congregation? Is he still an influential person in the lives of believers?

Denominational Traditions

To find some answers to the question of ministerial authority today, the Board of National Ministries, Presbyterian U.S., supported an interdenominational survey under the leadership of Hoyt Oliver, assistant professor of social science at Oxford College of Emory University, Oxford, Georgia. In the summer of 1967 Dr. Oliver received completed questionnaires from 179 ministers and 174 laymen of the following denominations: Presbyterian U.S., Presbyterian U.S.A., Methodists, Roman Catholic, Lutheran Church in America, Protestant Episcopal, Southern Baptist, Disciples of Christ. In addition, three groups of church laymen were interviewed for one or two hours, and seven ministers of different denominations were interviewed for thirty minutes to one hour. The questionnaires were distributed throughout the United States. The interviews were held with groups and ministers in Georgia.

Information from this survey should be viewed as exploratory rather than definitive, for the 353 questionnaires represented only 22 percent of all those which were mailed to ministers and laymen. Although the findings should be viewed with this caution, the survey did follow the denominational trends and images of the ministry found in the larger (10,000) and more representative Danforth Foundation Ministries Study of Dr.

Jeffrey Hadden, with which Dr. Oliver was in close contact. Dr. Hadden's conclusions are presented in *The Gathering Storm in the Churches.*[1]

The first finding of Dr. Oliver's study was the consensus of ministers and laymen that pastoral authority meant "*man* of God." A transcendent power had to be communicated through a human personality. The meaning of "man of God" varied with denominational tradition and with emphasis upon supernatural or natural operations of religion.

The denominational traditions of authority varied from Baptist and Disciples on one end of a continuum to Episcopalians and Catholics on the other end. The general emphases were as follows:

A special calling: Baptists, Methodists

Authority of Scripture and interpretation of the Word: Disciples, Presbyterians, Lutherans

Apostolic and sacramental authority: Roman Catholic, Episcopalian

Pastoral office: Lutheran

There certainly was no *one* source of authority which was stressed by respondents from all denominations. But within each tradition there seemed to be general agreement between ministers and laymen on definitions of the ministry and authority. Roman Catholic priests and laity alike mentioned ordination and apostolic authority. Disciples ministers and laymen emphasized scriptural interpretation. Southern Baptists emphasized calling by God four times more than they checked "or-

[1] (New York: Doubleday & Company, 1968).

dination," whereas Episcopalians and Roman Catholics checked "ordination" twice as often as they marked "calling." Other denominations in the sample mentioned "calling" two or three times more often than "ordination."

The Spiritual Dimension

The authority of the minister was also defined in terms of the natural and supernatural understanding of religion. The supernatural emphasis was given more by laymen and the natural emphasis more by ministers.

The laymen had a "spiritual" concept of the minister that is close to the tradition described in the previous chapter. They expected the minister to live a personal life of continuing relationship with God. They expected him to be a spiritual guide and moral example. They depended upon him in times of crisis such as illness, death, and doubt. Here the minister had authority.

But the laymen did not see the minister as an authority in such matters as a decision about work or career, political action, community involvement, emotional anxiety and stress.[2]

These answers are probably conditioned by the particular type of layman who answered the questionnaire.

[2] These are the answers of middle-class white men. Their conception of the minister is similar to the large (8,554 respondents) survey of the United Church of Christ by Yoshio Fukuyama. But 176 members of predominantly Negro United Churches of Christ saw the prophetic role as the primary emphasis of the clergy. Yoshio Fukuyama, "Parishioners' Attitudes Toward Issues in the Civil Rights Movement," mimeographed, 1967, p. 6.

They are lay leaders, and they may be lay leaders who are more "dedicated" than others who received the questionnaire but did not bother to answer it. Almost 50 percent were fifty years of age or older. Only 13 percent were under thirty. The interviews with church groups, who were generally young adults, revealed much more emphasis in natural as opposed to supernatural means of grace.

What are these natural and supernatural means of grace? These are distinctions closely associated with the findings of Mr. Fred Kling in a study of theological students. In a 1959 research bulletin from the Educational Testing Service, Mr. Kling discussed the world view of some theological students who felt a sense of "special leading" toward the ministry. These men believed that their calling was unique, that God revealed himself to them in specific acts, that prayer and Bible reading were ways of knowing the will of God. Their belief was that God had a purpose for each individual life, and the goal in life was to surrender oneself to God so that the plan might be revealed and obeyed.

Other students followed "natural leading." They tended to look at the needs of the world, assess their own talents, and then decide that the ministry was one of the ways in which they might be able to meet the world's needs in God's name. They relied upon the counsel of friends and professionals. Events in their lives were stimuli to thinking rather than definite signs from God. They were not sure of any definite plan for their lives. What they did believe was that God had put them in the world with a mind which could evaluate the needs of the time and assess their ability to meet those needs. He had also given them a spirit of commitment with which they could serve him in one of a variety of callings.

The distinction between natural and supernatural turns on our understanding of the way in which God works in the world. Many of the laymen in Dr. Oliver's study thought that God worked very specifically through chosen instruments of his, who would be in continuing relationship to God through prayer and Bible study. Many ministers shared this view, but they were more willing to use natural means of showing God's grace among men. That is, they had learned to listen and reflect in visitation, to use various psychological techniques, and to refer people to other sources of help more than laymen realized or expected of them.

If we were to pursue this study further, we would probably find that these two points of view are not confined exclusively to minister versus layman. As we have already shown from the study of the investigations of Mr. Kling, there are divisions among young clergymen on the way in which God works through their lives and in the world. There is also some evidence that a similar division of opinion is to be found among church members. When Phillip E. Hammond studied twelve Congregational churches in seven cities, he developed some categories similar to the supernatural and natural ones that we have presented. He found some laymen, and some churches, in which "traditionalism" was paramount. Here the emphasis was upon a community of the saved with a minister who held "special authority."

There were other laymen and churches with a "modernism" tradition, in which the church was considered primarily as a denomination and the minister was a person "with special training." [3]

The Ideal Image

Some differences between laymen and ministers also appear in expectations of the church and its ministry. Laymen emphasize the individual's relationship to God. The church is a means to this end and exists to meet persons' religious needs. The church is considered to be holy and not to be compared with other human institutions. It should help members live a Christian life rather than get involved in the problems of society.

Ministers agree more among themselves that the church is the "body of Christ," a fellowship of saints. They see the mission of the church to be help for persons to lead a more abundant life and prepare for service to the world. They believe that Christians should work through social organizations rather than setting up more church agencies. Ministers also believe that many churchgoers are using religion to escape their responsibility in the world. They do not see the institutional forms of the church as being especially sacred.

The laymen see the church more with a halo than the ministers do. At the same time, both groups see the church first of all as a community of the followers of

[3] Phillip E. Hammond, "Contemporary Protestant Ideology: A Typology of Church Images," *Review of Religious Research*, II (Spring, 1961), 161-70.

Jesus and agree that the church was established by God through Christ and his apostles.

Laymen think of the church as a very spiritual institution, but this does not mean that they expect the minister to be a holy-other or aloof individual. Instead, their expectations are of a warm individual who has expert advice to offer or healing to mediate. They compare the minister most favorably to a friend, a teacher, a doctor, or a father. They do not think of him as the chosen representative of a group who has direct power over them. Laymen reject the minister as being close to their expectations of a judge, president, or elected official of the government.

The layman's view of what a minister should be is very close to what ministers say they enjoy doing, according to the Danforth Ministry Survey.[4] Preaching, evangelism, pastoral counseling, Bible study, and prayer are these activities.

The Pastoral Ministry

If the minister to most laymen is little more than God's friendly representative, what place does he have in their personal lives? The answer to this question shows some agreement between the activities that ministers say they are doing and the expectations of their activities by laymen.

At the top of the list are times of celebration and crisis. Ministers and laymen gave priority to visitation

[4] See Hoyt P. Oliver, "Professional Authority and the Protestant Ministry: A Study of an Occupational Image," Chapter 6.

of the sick and lonely, help in understanding the Christian faith, baptism and reception of church members, conduct of funerals and comfort for the bereaved, preparation for marriage, direction of church lay workers. At the bottom of both lists are social and political action, advice on work and career decisions, community relations and needs, and physical needs.

Laymen would like a minister to visit when there is death in the home, physical illness, family trouble, serious moral problems, or doubts about the Christian faith. In contrast, a layman would go to some other professional person if he were faced with a "worldly" problem such as financial need, physical or mental illness, uncertainty about work or career, or a decision about community action.

A minister is not expected to have the skill and resources necessary to deal with the problems of the world. Instead, laymen expect the minister to use prayer, ask for God's guidance, and live the kind of life that would be exemplary. During the visit the minister is expected to give warm support and comfort, to be accepting and to offer "spiritual" advice. Neither ministers nor laymen think of this "spiritual" advice as judgment on a person's sin or exhortation to repentance, except in the case of four of the six Roman Catholic priests who were included in the study.

Just what picture does the minister have of himself in relation to the people who need his help? A variety of styles emerged from a correlation of answers given by the ministers:

The *pietist* would use various means of grace, listen,

remind of the teachings of Jesus, help work out practical plans, use insights from Scripture, relate some of his own experiences. He would be most at home with traditional religious methods.

The *reflector* would offer warm support and acceptance, listen and reflect, remind of the teachings of Jesus, and relate some of his own experiences. He would be essentially "nondirective."

The *evangelist-moralist* would remind of the teachings of Jesus, look for community resources, help work out practical plans, use insights from Scripture, and suggest proved moral standards.

The *resource man* would help in self-examination for commitment, remind persons of our great beliefs, focus on specific problems and plans, and speak judgments or urge repentance.

The *personalist* would assure that people are able to deal with their own problems, find support and acceptance in the church, speak of the way in which rituals express the mystery of God's care, and call upon other professional and community resources when necessary.

The *pragmatist* would focus on specific problems, help the persons to work out practical plans, encourage them to practice penitence and confession, and generally determine the method by the type of person being interviewed.

The *liturgist* would use means of grace such as worship and the sacraments and join with persons in these mysteries of God's care.

The Minister's Choice

Ministers are not being consulted about many of the major decisions of life, but they are welcomed when there are personal difficulties. This places some definite restrictions upon the minister's authority. We might classify these restrictions in terms of some of the sociological categories on role theory that were introduced in Chapter 1. The minister is expected to be heard in two areas: the maintenance of the pattern of worship and belief and the integration of the interpersonal relationships of church members. He is not expected to be a power in the mission of the church in changing the lives of men in the world or the organization of the church to focus upon specific social action.

The problem for the minister is not to set any one of these functions against the other but to utilize all four of them. This will mean that he must extend his own and the layman's understanding of the areas in which the minister can exercise authority and that he must develop facility as an expert in each of these areas. This calls for a clear knowledge of values (pattern maintenance), sensitivity to feelings and relationships (integration), judicious use of power (goal achievement), and persuasive change of motivation (adaptation).[5]

The goal of the minister's authority would be this, to

[5] For other investigations and discussions of the role theory of the ministry in relation to laymen and clergy, see W. W. Shroeder, "Lay Expectations of the Ministerial Role," *Journal for the Scientific Study of Religion*, II (April, 1963), 217-27; Theodore E. Evans, "The Brethren Pastor," *ibid.*, III (October, 1963), 42-51; Samuel Klausner, "Role Adaptation of Pastors and Psychiatrists," *ibid.*, IV (October, 1964), 14-39.

demonstrate transcendent power through his personal relations without letting his own personality get in the way. Laymen are expecting personal rather than official authority, and that personal authority is to be "spiritual."

The last word is in quotation marks because it is not quite the meaning of spiritual in the New Testament. The element of judgment is missing. The minister is expected to be a man of God, but he had better be a friendly one!

5
The Characteristics
of Manly Authority

The minister is to be "spiritual" and personal. In the nineteenth century this was defined as a concern for the conversion of souls.[1] In the twentieth century laymen and ministers see pastoral authority as the friendly presentation of God's concern and guidance for people in doubt or difficulty. The minister is accepted as an authority when he demonstrates godly character and communicates the presence of a power beyond himself. Exactly how is this authority communicated to individuals? Is the "friendly pastor" respected when he is soft and reassuring? Is he always to wait for people to raise problems with him, or does he take the initiative in seeking them out? And how does he structure the conversation so that the "spiritual" element will appear?

In seeking answers to these questions, we turn from the essentially sociological, role-defining investigations

[1] Mead, in Niebuhr and Williams, *The Ministry in Historical Perspectives*, p. 229.

of the previous chapter to a psychologically oriented case study.

In this chapter we will explore the characteristics of a *man* of God. In the next chapter we will consider the abuses and opportunities of pastoral initiative toward people in need.

The Characteristics of a Man of God

A pastor's power is personal, but it is not power in himself; it is the representation of the God whom he serves. The minister must convey transcendent authority through human relationships.

What are the qualities within a man and in his relationships that command respect? To answer this question, I looked over the verbatim conversation-sequence interviews of theological students with mental hospital patients during a summer of clinical theological education. In a group of twelve students, three were evaluated by their theological supervisors as men who took responsibilities well and presented themselves firmly as counselors. The supervisors' reports stated that they worked consistently under heavy pressure, were aggressive without being hostile, and were well organized in their pastoral sense of direction and purpose. They had good relationships with hospital personnel and understood their patients. They were accepted as "*men* of God."

Three other students had consistent problems with authority. The supervisor reported that they were obsequious or evasive. One of the three was unable to get beyond the "handshaking" stage of visitation. The other two listened passively to what they were told and tried to apply pastoral techniques without understanding. One supervisor characterized them as "boyish." Their personal and pastoral identity was undeveloped or inhibited.

Each of the students had written approximately fifty verbatim interviews with patients in a state mental hospital. For the purposes of this study the interviews of the students who were considered by their supervisors to be mature were compared with the interviews of those who appeared to be immature. As the three hundred interviews were read, the characteristics of the mature pastors were listed first. In subsequent reading of the immature interviews the opposite of these characteristics began to appear. The final list was of four interrelated qualities.

The characteristics of manly authority were (1) personal commitment, (2) realistic judgment, (3) direct conversation, (4) understanding relations with patients and personnel. These qualities meshed. As the subsequent illustrations will show, all four were part of an adequate demonstration of manly authority. In contrast, an immature minister might exhibit one of these qualities without the balancing maturity of the other three. Thus commitment without realism was naïveté; directness without understanding was harshness or hostility.

Personal Commitment

There were both firmness and tenderness in the commitment of the "men of God" to their patients. Some-

times this appeared in relevant observations. These and
other quoted materials are altered excerpts from the verbatim reports.

Mrs. M. was in a meditative mood. She had little to say as
I moved about the hall. Finally I came back to her place and
said, "Mrs. M., you seem to be a bit preoccupied today." She
answered, "I showed a letter to the doctor. He said I cannot
leave until I have finished my treatments." I replied that
this must be very disappointing to her. I did not know the
doctor that she had mentioned.

At other times the commitment might be more dra-
matic. On one occasion a patient became very disturbed while talking to his student pastor. The patient's
eyes became glassy, and his body shook. The student
reported, "I felt my mouth open and become tight. But
I put my hand on his shoulder so that I might have
some contact with him. I called him by name. I felt
anxiety, helplessness, futility, sympathy, and compas-
sion." In a few seconds the patient had recovered his
composure. The student admitted to his supervisor that
he was frightened by the experience; yet he had determined that he would "stand by his patient."

Sympathetic commitment might appear as an obser-
vation about a patient's point of view and a statement
of the student's own position:

PATIENT: The Spirit is like breath.
CHAPLAIN: That's close to the meaning of the term.
PATIENT: If I hold my breath, I can hold back the Spirit?
CHAPLAIN: How do you mean?

PATIENT: If I hold my breath, I can stop time.

CHAPLAIN: If you hold your breath, you may not be able to tell what time it is, but that wouldn't stop time for me. When we talk about the Spirit and refer to breath, this is just a way of talking about it. Would you tell me why you are interested in this?

On one occasion a commitment called for a strictly man-to-man approach. One of the more adequate students was approached by a patient who was described by the student as "extractive." The student sought to offer "a nonthreatening relationship with a male authority figure":

CHAPLAIN: The doctors have the final responsibility for the patient, Mr. C. I might be glad to take you for a walk, but if something should happen, then the doctor would be responsible. Why don't you ask Dr. A. if you could take this walk?

PATIENT: Well, I will do that when he comes around. Dr. R. says that I have criminal charges against me. (He looks me straight in the eye.) I'm here because I murdered a man. (He continues to look for my reaction.)

CHAPLAIN: (I keep a steady look at his eyes and pause.) I know that, Mr. C.

PATIENT: I can't remember doing it. I don't remember anything about it.

Because these ministers were adequate authorities, they were able to discuss the problem of moral authority with their patients:

PATIENT: The Lord has been very good to me, and I know he has helped me in getting well. I talked to one of the other chaplains about hearing the voices of Jesus and God. You know about that too. Those don't come anymore now. It was something so very unusual.

CHAPLAIN: Well, I am interested in this. And now that the voices have stopped, particularly Jesus and God telling you what is right, how do you know what is the right thing to do now?

PATIENT: Well, I know God's Word, and I can tell what I am doing wrong.

These interviews showed personal interest and support that were firm and realistic.

In contrast, the immature ministers often failed to offer any support to their patients:

CHAPLAIN: I guess no matter how old a guy gets, his mother still thinks of him as "Sonny." This seems to be true with my mother, too.

PATIENT: Yeah, she calls my sister "Daughter."

CHAPLAIN: Your mother mentioned that she doesn't get out too much anymore. How old is she?

PATIENT: She is about sixty-three. She has been living alone since my father died. He died when I was small. He had heart trouble. We found him dead in bed one morning.

CHAPLAIN: How old was he when he died?

The chaplain asked other questions about the difference in age between mother and father, the relationship between the mother and the father, and then moved on to discuss storms in New York City. When the student was asked to evaluate the interview, he missed his lack of tenderness toward the patient and complained instead that the patient would not say many deep things about his life experiences.

In place of personal commitment, one of the immature students substituted stereotyped answers:

> PATIENT: Do you worry about things like I do? I worry about the Communists, do you?
>
> CHAPLAIN: Why do you worry about them?
>
> PATIENT: They might start a war and destroy the world.
>
> CHAPLAIN: Mrs. H., I think God is bigger than the Communists. He won't let the world be destroyed until he is ready. The whole situation is in the hands of God.

When these students did offer support, it was superficial or compelled. For example, after a profane and verbose patient had harangued the chaplain for half an hour, he told the chaplain that he was sure God would forgive him and send him to heaven. The chaplain replied, "You have a strong faith, Mr. R., and I'm glad that you have told me about it." Or a patient would talk the chaplain into agreeing with him, as in the following:

> PATIENT: If Jesus healed the lame and the blind people before, he can do it again, can't he?
>
> CHAPLAIN: You believe that, Mr. F.?
>
> PATIENT: Sure I do, don't you, brother?
>
> CHAPLAIN: Why, yes, I do.

Instead of realistic commitment, these ministers offered agreement when they were coerced and superficial reassurance when they were anxious.

Realistic Judgment

The presentation of reality was closely connected with the issue of personal support and commitment. Manly pastors conveyed the world as it is with tenderness. They were matter-of-fact rather than sentimental in facing issues with patients. They tended to look at things *with* the patients rather than apart from or against the patients.

Sometimes reality would appear naturally in a "commonsense suggestion":

PATIENT: My second wife has really changed things around. She makes up my mind and changes it several times a day. If I ever get out of here, it is going to be different. I will have nothing to do with her. I do not even want her to know where I am.

CHAPLAIN: Are you divorced from her?

PATIENT: No, but she mentioned something about this one time. She said she wanted to marry the man that she was with at that time.

CHAPLAIN: Don't you think it would be an idea to clear that up?

PATIENT: Yes, but I'll try to do it without seeing her.

A chaplain might think with a patient and still jolt him when the healthy reality of the chaplain's perception was measured against the sick distortions of the patient:

CHAPLAIN: Why is the Great Mother important for you?

PATIENT: Well, you see, I have been martyred many times in my life; I have given up my life many times. The last time I remember before I came here was getting off a merchant ship. I had given up my life, and I had been cut up in pieces many times in my life.

CHAPLAIN: How do you explain the fact that you are still here and in one piece?

PATIENT: (He looks bewildered.) I don't know. All those who are under me have gone down below. I sent all the jury down below. . . . We are all born by one Great Mother. One time I was you and you were me.

CHAPLAIN: I don't believe that is true.

PATIENT: Then you don't believe the same religion I do. Will you give me a Bible?

CHAPLAIN: No.

PATIENT: Why?

CHAPLAIN: Because I don't think the Bible is something to play games with.

PATIENT: But it does me good. Wouldn't you want to play games if you had been given life and twenty-one years?

CHAPLAIN: Are you just trying to get a Bible from me because you think a chaplain has to give you a Bible?

PATIENT: I have to get merit to be better than the others. I want to get above them.

CHAPLAIN: Then the only thing about other people is that you can get something from them, is that it?

PATIENT: (He hesitated here; it seemed as if no one had

ever put the question to him so bluntly.) I have to get up above.

The immature students never seemed to grasp the reality of their world or its relationship to the patient's world. Their attempts to "set things straight" seemed ineffectual:

CHAPLAIN: Do you feel that you are the only patient on this hall who is saved?

PATIENT: Yeah, my father wants me to get out where I should be.

CHAPLAIN: Who is your father?

PATIENT: The man upstairs. The overhead man.

CHAPLAIN: If he is your father, can he be my father too?

PATIENT: I don't know anything about that. He will forgive me for anything that I do.

CHAPLAIN: Is that what the Bible means when it talks about love? Doesn't it say that God wants us to love him and our neighbors?

PATIENT: That's in your Bible; it's not in my Bible.

CHAPLAIN: What kind of Bible do you have?

PATIENT: My Bible doesn't have fighting in it.

CHAPLAIN: Do you have the Old Testament or the New Testament?

PATIENT: My Bible has none of that stuff.

In the continuation of the interview the chaplain could not find out the patient's name from her. Finally, in exasperation, he stated his name and the fact that he was chaplain on this hall. When the patient said that she did not need a preacher, the chaplain responded,

"I didn't say you needed a preacher, did I?" This definiteness on his part brought a smile from the patient and her only definite response on a feeling level. It was his only response on a feeling level, too.

Another chaplain could not handle the reality of illness and its relation to the outside world. As was his custom, he solved the problem by presenting a stereotype:

PATIENT: Those people outside are crazier than I am.
CHAPLAIN: There are a lot of people who are not in here.
PATIENT: I know that, but a lot of them ought to be in here. If they all were here, this would be some nut house. This is about the worst place you can be.
CHAPLAIN: Yes, it's a bad place, but there are some worse places than this. Jail is a pretty bad place.

When this same chaplain tried to be realistic, he lacked tenderness in his attempt. His interview with a bedridden patient began on a very "realistic" note. The patient was told by the aide that she had been in the same room for nine months. The patient looked at the chaplain in surprise and said, "Is that reality?" The chaplain's answer was, "She's been here longer than I have," as he looked at the attendant. Later in the conversation the patient asked for prayer that she might get well. The chaplain replied, "Well, let me ask you this: Suppose God does not heal you; what then?" Then he went on to ask if she would accept God's will whatever it might be; would she trust in God if he did not answer her prayers if they wanted him to; could the patient trust in God among patients who were sicker than she was? Having satisfied himself concerning all these conditions, the chaplain offered his prayer.

The responses of the immature students indicated that they had no sure grasp of reality for themselves or anyone else. The mature students seemed to know what the world was about. They not only could make their own way in it, but they could offer appropriate and understanding comments for the benefit of others who were not so sure of themselves. When some of these contrasts were pointed out to one of the less adequate students, he replied, "Well, why hasn't anyone told me about these things before?" This was said in hurt amazement rather than in open anger.

Direct Conversation

Directness and forcefulness, tempered by a concern for patients, were further distinctives of the ministers who were mature authorities. These men were bold to remove obstacles. They did not use hostile or aggressive emotions to keep patients away from them. One of the chaplains, for example, was forthright in recognizing that some patients did not prefer to talk with him:

CHAPLAIN: How are you getting along today? I am afraid I don't remember your name.
PATIENT: F. Charles F. We met the other day.
CHAPLAIN: Yes, I recall, but I could not remember your name. I wanted to stop by and get better acquainted with you today, Mr. F.

PATIENT: I don't know if I want to talk to any preacher.
CHAPLAIN: Well, that's all right. Not everyone wants to talk to a preacher, and there is nothing that says you have to. (I started to move away. He straightened up abruptly and began to talk in a belligerent tone.)
PATIENT: I can't talk to anybody around here. They think I am blind, that I don't know anything. I know what they're trying to keep me here for—they can't fool me.
CHAPLAIN: Why do you think you are being kept here, Mr. F.?

As the interview continued, the chaplain recognized that he was becoming hostile toward the patient and at the same time the patient was hostile toward him. In the evaluation the chaplain stated that the "cocksureness and closed mind" of the patient made the chaplain angry. By the end of the interview he did not want to talk to the patient, but at least he began the interview by recognizing that the patient might not want to talk to him.

On another occasion the chaplain was direct and more consistently even in his temperament. During the family conference the mother of a patient stated:

MRS. B.: Well, you are a preacher. You ought to know whether or not it is right for anyone to be married twice. I believe that it is wrong. His (pointing at her husband) first wife is still living.
CHAPLAIN: (Rather sternly) Are you saying that you think it was wrong for your husband to get married again, Mrs. B.?

MRS. B.: Yes, I believe it was, and that's why we have all this trouble now. God is punishing us.

CHAPLAIN: If you thought it was wrong, Mrs. B., why did you marry him?

MRS. B.: Well, I guess I was young and foolish and didn't know what I was doing.

MR. B.: Do you see, preacher, what I have to put up with? (Husband and wife then began to make accusations against each other and many threats.)

CHAPLAIN: Now, just a minute, both of you. I am not here to listen to your arguments or to act as a referee. My purpose as a minister is to understand your son's problem and to assure you that in spite of your fears and impatience the hospital is doing everything possible to help him. (Couple quieted down and directed their questions to me.)

A direct statement was sometimes motivated by a social concern; as a moral authority the chaplain wished to increase the patient's ethical sensitivity. For example:

CHAPLAIN: Now, how have things been going for you since you have come to the hospital?

PATIENT: All right, except that there's no one to talk to. These nuts don't remember anything from one moment to the next. It's almost impossible to carry on a sensible conversation with them.

CHAPLAIN: How do you think they feel when you call them that?

PATIENT: (He looks confused.) They don't remember things from one moment to the next. Where are you from? (The patient then began to boast about his accomplishments as a professional gambler.)

In contrast, a lack of sensitive directness seemed to be one of the major deficiencies of the chaplains who had an immature identity.

The immature chaplains could be told to "define limits," "allow the patient to carry his own anxiety," or "be direct in defining your role." But the supervisors might have been better advised to keep silent, for the results were not satisfactory. After two months of reminders that patients were walking over him, one student took the following "stand":

CHAPLAIN: You wanted to see me, Mrs. S.?

PATIENT: Yes, I did. (Emphatically and elevated) I want you to call my sister-in-law and have her tell my husband to come and see me.

CHAPLAIN: Mrs. S., I am a chaplain . . .

PATIENT: (Breaking in) I know that you are a chaplain and . . .

CHAPLAIN: (Breaking in) Mrs. S., do you think that making phone calls is part of my job? That is a job for the social worker. Have you talked with him?

PATIENT: I have never seen a social worker on this hall. All I want is for my husband to come and get me out of here.

CHAPLAIN: That's a job for the social worker. Ask Miss J. to call him.

PATIENT: She's not working today.

CHAPLAIN: Then get the aide to help you.

PATIENT: I want my husband to come and get me out of here.

CHAPLAIN: That is not my job. I want to be your chaplain, but you need a social worker to help you with this problem. If you want a chaplain, feel free to call on me.

PATIENT: (Calling after the chaplain as he walks away) I want to get out of here and go back and see my children.

In his evaluation of this interview the chaplain stated that he did not care if he ever saw this patient again or not. He felt that she was very manipulative, and he said he would not talk with her again unless she asked for an interview. At the time his feelings were much like those of the chaplain mentioned above who had been angered by a patient. The difference was that the chaplain with a strong identity was willing to carry through the interview and returned to see the patient again. The more immature student was ready to quit as soon as he was aware of his hostility toward a patient.

Sometimes it appeared that the immature chaplains could not be direct because of their overwhelming desire to be accepted by patients at any cost. On the rare occasions when they disagreed with a patient, they were anxious to make sure that the "relationship was not broken."

CHAPLAIN: Well, Mrs. L., I am afraid I just can't agree with you here. Regardless of how we look at ourselves, I believe that God loves us. I believe that he loves you.

PATIENT: Well, then, you are a preacher (laughs).

CHAPLAIN: (Laughing, too) You're right about that. But just because we disagree doesn't keep us from being friends, does it?

PATIENT: No, we can be friends (pause), but I don't see how God can love everyone, especially sinners. . . .

CHAPLAIN: Is there something that you want to do and you can't do it?

PATIENT: Yes, it's on my chart. If you have not read it, you can.

CHAPLAIN: I guess I could, but I'd rather have you tell me. I'd like to think you had enough confidence in me as your friend to tell me.

PATIENT: Oh, no, there are so many of us. I would just get lost in the shuffle.

CHAPLAIN: Now, I will have to disagree with you again, Mrs. L., because I am concerned about you. (The chaplain then made a good attempt to move the patient toward a discussion of a problem that she had mentioned previously, her estrangement from her husband. The patient would not talk about this, and so the chaplain commented about her crochet work in occupational therapy.) Crochet work is terribly hard, isn't it? I asked my mother to show me once when I was a little boy, but I never could learn. I got the thread all tangled up.

The "directness" of these chaplains usually took the form of stereotyped phrases asked near the beginning of each interview. "Tell me about yourself" was the typical starter for one chaplain; "Where is your church?" was the invariable question of another.

When the immature students made direct statements, they were not balanced by feelings for the patient. One patient tried to explain the meaning of faith to one of these chaplains. The chaplain turned this into an argument on the relative value of magician's power versus the power of faith. His responses began with phrases such as "I don't think" or "Don't you think." He wanted to make his points rather than clear away the debris that would allow him to see the patient's thinking more clearly.

One of the features of misused directness was the advice given by immature chaplains. This usually consisted of vague generalizations. There were moral overtones that the chaplain was right and that the patient was wrong unless he gave assent:

CHAPLAIN: Do you think your husband and children love you?

PATIENT: Yes, I think that they do.

CHAPLAIN: Don't you think it does them good to know that you can be seen and talked to? Don't you think it does them good to know that they can come to see you? And think of your husband; don't you think he would be lost if he couldn't come every Sunday to see you?

PATIENT: Yes, I suppose so.

CHAPLAIN: Do you still have any faith in God? Suffering tests our faith and patience. This is the way we become mature Christians.

PATIENT: Yes, I guess that's so.

CHAPLAIN: It surely is.

Understanding Relationships

The ministers with well-formed authority were more active than the other chaplains in making suggestions to patients, but they were not of the "bad advice" category that has just been mentioned. Instead, they had a sureness of interpretation and an aggressive desire to capture the full significance of an issue or to lead through a difficult problem to a deeper level of understanding. For example, during one of the family conferences reported on at the beginning of the previous section, the chaplain stated to the patient's mother:

CHAPLAIN: Then you did recognize that your son really did need help because he was sick?

MRS. B.: Yes, sir. But the hospital staff don't seem to think I know anything about it and don't believe that what I tell them will happen.

CHAPLAIN: Mrs. B., correct me if I do not understand you clearly, but I sensed the other day and I see it again today that you do not really think the hospital is helping your son. Is this so?

MRS. B.: Well, I guess they are doing all they can, but he isn't getting any better.

CHAPLAIN: I can surely appreciate that it is most difficult to be patient. Especially when your son is not improving as quickly as you had expected him to. Therefore, you do not trust the hospital staff, is that it?

MRS. B.: Yes, and I will tell you why I don't trust them.

The understanding chaplain often took the initiative in presenting an idea that might help a patient express significant feeling:

CHAPLAIN: While you were helping your mother, did you ever think you would like to get away from it all? To not have to do all this housework?

PATIENT: Oh, I have thought about getting away from

here. If I could get somebody good to stay with, I would. But I don't know who that would be.

CHAPLAIN: It would be nice to get away from here. But I was wondering if you felt this way at home with your mother. Did you ever feel you would like to be free, to get away for yourself?

PATIENT: I was afraid I would get a mean man. I didn't want that.

In this instance the chaplain firmly returned the conversation to the patient's feeling about her mother, when the patient was attempting to move it away to less threatening areas such as when she could get out of the hospital.

This same chaplain was skillful in helping other patients to come close to some hard thoughts:

PATIENT: The nurses do take good care of me, but if my family won't come without being called, I don't want them called.

CHAPLAIN: You mentioned that several of your family have a lot of work at home and it is difficult for them to get away. I am sure they do want to know when you are ill and would like to be called. This is the only way they can find out when you are not well.

PATIENT: I don't know.

CHAPLAIN: We do have our families, and sometimes they do forget us in times like these. Sometimes it is hard for us to accept our feelings toward them when they treat us this way. We may become angry toward them sometimes.

PATIENT: Oh, I am not angry toward them. Only they should care a little bit (long pause).

The ability to take initiative at an appropriate moment and to offer a sensitive interpretation were characteristic of mature authority. The interviews of this type seemed to be between two persons who cared about each other but who had some idea as to who they were. Both patient and chaplain appeared at their best in these moments:

CHAPLAIN: You seem to be low these days, Mrs. M.

PATIENT: Yes, chaplain, things are building up again. But this hall gets on my nerves, and I have got to get away.

CHAPLAIN: Everything seems to build up, and then you feel low? What do you do when this happens?

PATIENT: Well, I worked in the dining room and just collapsed one day. Now I paint chairs, and sometimes I help to wash patients and get them ready for occupational therapy. It also helped one time to talk with a doctor. I told him all the things I felt, and then I was embarrassed.

CHAPLAIN: Do you feel embarrassed when you talk to me?

PATIENT: No, you seem to understand. The doctor told me I could go to my sister's house, but I do not know if they will come for me or not.

CHAPLAIN: How do you think you will do if you go to your sister's house? Last time we talked you had some doubts about it.

PATIENT: It will be all right if they don't try to marry me off. They're always introducing me to someone and expecting him to marry me. The way my husband treated me, I don't want to get married again.

CHAPLAIN: Do you think all men are like your husband?

PATIENT: My doctor said the same thing to me. I am afraid of men; every time I see one, I want to run.

CHAPLAIN: In which direction?
PATIENT: (She laughs at this.) You know what I mean, chaplain. You know what married people do. My husband treated me badly in that way.
CHAPLAIN: You felt he just used you sexually, is that it?
PATIENT: Yes, and I get this feeling whenever I see a man. I can't trust them. I suppose it could be me.

The sharpest contrast in all these interviews was between the type of interview that has just been mentioned and some of the interpretations without insight that were offered by the immature chaplains. Here is an example:

PATIENT: My husband does not want me around. I am half dead. (She points to her paralyzed limbs.)
CHAPLAIN: You get around pretty well for a person that's half dead. Just because you're paralyzed, that doesn't mean you are half dead. Think of the people who can't get around as well as you do.
PATIENT: Yes, but I am half dead, and I am going to die.
CHAPLAIN: Well, we are all going to do that. You look to me like you are not anywhere near doing that yet.

The most boyish of the chaplains would slide away from opportunities to relate present statements of patients to previous statements, or to connect their promises to reality. After nine interviews with a patient he could offer no more than this:

PATIENT: When I say I'm not going to take a drink, I won't take one. (Patient has a long history of problems with alcoholic beverages.)

CHAPLAIN: You're always able to keep promises you make?
PATIENT: Oh, yes. And anyway, I wouldn't go to my sister's when I was under the influence of alcohol.
CHAPLAIN: What would your sister say if you did?
PATIENT: She wouldn't like it—she could tell right away if I had anything to drink.

The chaplain then asked additional questions which directed the patient toward his doctor, who could tell him whether or not he could visit his sister. In his evaluation the student correctly saw that the patient needed to develop more confidence in himself which could be verified in experience. But I wonder how this can be developed by a minister who does not yet have confidence in himself as an authority?

The Incarnation of the Spirit

With this personal and perplexing question about mature identity, we come back to the quotation from Daniel Day Williams, that personal authority "arises out of the concrete incarnation of the spirit of loving service which by God's help becomes present in the care of souls."

In this chapter we have tested the theological proposition that the competence of the minister is measured by his ability to incarnate godly concern for others and convey this realistically to others. We have found that the clinical elements of this assertion are commitment, judgment, directness, understanding. These are qualities we see in mature men of God and do not see in less mature men.

From these interviews it appears that a "friendly pastor" would be uncomfortable with people who have serious emotional problems. Softness and reassurance become superficiality and anxious compliance in the immature chaplain. The characteristic of mature chaplains is quiet assurance, not reassurance.

Mature ministers in these interviews were willing to take some risks for the sake of the patient. They could be direct, even aggressive, in challenging sick thinking and unethical attitudes. They were understanding and patient, but they were not passive. Sometimes they were frightened or anxious, but they stayed with the patients.

The incarnation of concern among mature ministers was a combination of discipleship and craftsmanship. They committed the best they had to the people under their care and used their counseling skills to meet sick people with a healthy point of view. In biblical language, they spoke the truth with "love and self-control" (II Tim. 1:7).

A well-trained and committed minister would soon shake the assertion of laymen in Chapter 4 that ministers are not authorities in time of emotional anxiety and stress. The laymen might reply that they would like to see such ministers, but they have not met any. I believe that the vital answer is with the clergyman. If he is as immature as some men in this study, he will be seldom consulted about personal problems. But if he is as mature and skillful as some of the other chaplains, he will be a concrete incarnation of loving concern to those in distress.

6
Boldness in Pastoral Counseling

Some ministers would be willing to stop with the last section of Chapter 5. So long as they incarnate concern, they feel that their mission is accomplished. And with severely disturbed people that may be a realistic goal in contacts of a few months' duration. Some persons have been so inhibited or starved emotionally that they cannot respond with the warmth, appreciation, and acceptance that an adequate minister expresses to them. They have been so decimated by life that words like love, forgiveness, and reconciliation are almost without meaning. They have no wholesome memories to go with feeling-laden phrases like "God is love." So we must *be* love to these people before we can speak of God specifically.

But the tragic circumstances of mental illness do not set the limits for all personal ministries. I saw this vividly when I moved from the chaplaincy of a mental hospital to the pastorate of a suburban congregation. Many of the suburbanites were able and willing to be themselves. They were adequate people. Consequently, they talked freely and quickly about specific, realistic issues in their lives. And they responded with trust to my open concern, questioning, advice, objection, or assurance. They could be transparent selves, and they liked a minister who could be himself.

The ministry of reconciliation proceeded on a different level with these adequate people. They needed to be challenged because they were "self-actualized," because they could get most of what they wanted in this life. It took aggressive action to show some of them a power beyond themselves.

"Aggressiveness" sounds the note of hostility to some people. They equate it with "attack." A more consistent word with the Christian spirit would be "boldness." Boldness in pastoral counseling is the free expression to an individual of godly concern for him or the community. It is an activation of God's love in a spirit of self-control.

The Rejection of Domination

There is always the possibility of self-deception in the use of boldness. It can easily become domination. So the pastoral epistles warn that the flock of God is not to be tended by constraint, but willingly (I Peter 5:3). Those who are in the Christian fellowship are enjoined to have "a tender heart and a humble mind" (I Peter 3:8). When we are humble, then the boldness is perceived to be of God alone (Acts 4:13-22).

Unfortunately, many ministers have neither the discipleship nor the craftsmanship to heed these admonitions. Here is an example of the blind leading the blind:

Pastor Snell was bewildered by his new suburban church. He had never met any "big businessmen" before; yet he found them to be leaders in this congregation. For a year Pastor Snell tried to preach "New Testament Christianity" as he had learned it in the rural Midwest. He could not tell if he was being accepted or not, until the evening of a special deacons' meeting. At this meeting Pastor Snell was surprised to hear a recommendation from the chairman of the deacons that a deacon should be admonished against secret meetings designed to undermine the fellowship of the church and confidence in the pastor. During the hour-and-a-half discussion that followed the pastor was surprised and horrified to hear the ways in which a small group of men had actively organized discontent in the congregation. Most of the deacons knew what had occurred and readily voted to censure the conduct of their colleague.

Two weeks later Pastor Snell was called by the sister of a dissatisfied deacon: "Preacher, my brother's wife has just been taken to a mental hospital. She has gone to pieces. Won't you please go by and see my brother?" Pastor Snell chose to go first to the hospital, where he was allowed a brief visit with the distraught wife. She told of many ways in which she felt tyrannized by her husband and troubled by his lack of consideration for others. "He always acts like he is right," she said.

The pastor was further bewildered by this conversation. After several days of intermittent thought on the subject, he told what he knew to a friend who was hold-ing a revival in a nearby church. Pastor Snell concluded the story with: "I have come to the conclusion that it is the judgment of God upon that whole family. That man has done terrible things to me, and I have tried to love in turn. God has dealt with him through his wife. God has protected me and put down those who trouble our church."

This is the kind of judgment that has been consistent-ly denounced in our generation by theologians, psychiatrists, psychologists, social workers, and pastoral counselors. It is denounced because it is judgment without understanding. Pastor Snell had such poor contact with his people and so little understanding of their feelings that he reacted with horror and surprise in the deacons' meeting. He knew so little about family relationships and emotional problems that he glossed over the years of conflict that led to a wife's mental ill-ness and concluded that her distraction was an instan-taneous act of God which followed disciplinary action upon her husband.

The minister's ignorance of men was bad enough. But in addition to this there was a lack of humility before God. The pastor pompously presumed that any-one who opposed him or his church program would be immediately punished by God. Fortunately, the pastor to whom he told this story warned against "presumptive pride." He told his friend that it was dangerous for any minister to think that he was so righteous that God would be his "hatchet man."

One answer to this abuse of boldness was the development of client-centered counseling among educated clergymen. A listening ministry was emphasized. Personal judgments were to be inhibited.

This method was a valuable check upon heavy-footed shepherds who rushed in to trample down the parishioner. It increased the sensitivity of the counselor to others and disciplined his need for self-satisfaction. Client-centered methods suppressed the anxiety of a beginning student to do something here and now or to make premature judgments.

Sensitivity to others, patience, and humility are the guiding virtues that I have found in this kind of pastoral counseling. Students learn to take account of another person's motivation and capacity to grow. The personal preference of the counselor and his urge to "do something" are held in check.

The Problem of Powerlessness

So long as client-centered techniques were used to correct abuses in pastoral counseling or to instruct students in one phase of their training, the ministry was strengthened. But many problems have arisen when client-centered theory and method have become the center of a pastor's counseling. The inherent passivity of "responsive" counseling troubles a pastor when he sees someone who is comfortable in a way of life that will soon lead him to destruction. How is he to "awaken" an individual who has no recognition of his need for God?

What is a pastor to do when he sees that an individual has some sense of need and cannot focus upon resources that would give him help? Should the pastor go beyond "reflection" to offer clues for an understanding of the situation?

There is also the problem of a pastor's values and opinions. Can he operate without judgments so long as he is a "shepherd" and then become a judge when he enters an administrative or organizational role?

Basic opinions are not suspendible. To a psychiatrist like Dr. Jerome Frank, consistent client-centered techniques are like brainwashing.[1] The client, like a prisoner, knows that something is wrong, but no one will tell him what it is. Desperately he seeks in his weekly sessions to find some clues by which he may find healing. Some clients finally learn that their anxiety can be relieved by talking of themselves. This brings approval from the counselor. So long as they submit to the counselor's hidden value system, they find acceptance, and often get better. Dr. Franck comments that psychiatrists have often used this technique of hiding themselves behind the mask of "responsiveness" and, when the patient rebels against this, he is accused of being "defensive."

It would be refreshing to note the ability of more psychiatrists and ministers to see the place of values and judgments in their professional conversations. But with the usual cultural lag, recessive counselors are still hiding behind "client-centered" phrases, while the psychologist who developed the concept, Carl Rogers, has

[1] Morris I. Stein, *Contemporary Psychotherapies* (Glencoe, Ill.: The Free Press, 1961), Chapter II.

moved on to an emphasis on congruence and authenticity.

Any counselor has some power. For the minister or psychologist it is the authority of personality (charisma) and expertness. The values held by powerful helping people are important, and they cannot be hidden. Why should they be? The more open they are, the easier it is for a parishioner or client to accept or reject them.

Some counselors reject this because their hidden power motives are so strong. They believe that if they tell someone what they think, the individual will give up his own ideas and submit to this overawing authority. So they argue, "You can't let a client know what you think. It would influence, intimidate, coerce him."

Sometimes the question pops out, "Do you want to *dominate* a person?" At times I do, but this usually is not accomplished by an open admission of my opinion. The best way to dominate in counseling is quietly to maneuver the client to ask the questions we think are important and then respond with interest only to the answers that we think we should give.

Ministers are really not as powerful personally as some think they are when they say, "Oh, I'd never reveal my opinion"—as if people would automatically accept their views. The problem for a skillful pastor is to admit how powerless he really is to change other people. Once he does this, he won't be so afraid of admitting how he feels when questions of values are raised by those who seek his counsel. We *can* express concern for others without dominating them.

The Snare of Deception

Of course, we might like to keep a little extra power in the form of confidential information. Then the minister would have great security. He would always know more than the person who confides in him. Thus he can retain some power. He may say that he is "serving" the person, but it's done with a certain secretness that smacks of duplicity.

The power motives come into the open when the minister, like some psychoanalysts, asserts that he "knows what is best" for his counselee. Dr. Kurt Eissler gave an example of this motivation in *The Psychiatrist and the Dying Patient*.[2] On one occasion the patient asked the psychiatrist if she were going to die. Dr. Eissler answered, "No." The patient said that she wanted to ask him because she knew he had the information from her medical specialist. She would have needed to get some financial affairs in order if she were to die soon. Since she trusted her psychiatrist, she believed that she would live longer because of his answer. In justifying this lie, Dr. Eissler said that the woman might have become psychotic if he had told her the truth. Yet, as disproof of rationale for deceit, the woman had managed her husband's estate in good order and withstood the psychological shock of several major operations.

Ministers may also practice duplicity because they fear the results of an open confrontation. In one instance a minister talked to a daughter as though he knew nothing about her dating of a divorced man. The

[2] (New York: International Universities Press, 1955), pp. 204-9.

minister told me that the mother sent him to see the daughter. He did not wish to admit openly to the daughter what was being said by mother and friends because "that community has some hard feelings toward anyone who is divorced, and I don't want to get mixed up in it."

Frequently, duplicity is seen in the minister who uses information on a resistant counselee. He begins the interview with a bland "What do you feel that you'd like to talk about?" If he doesn't get to the "problem," he begins to ask questions that insinuate his foreknowledge. Or he may seek to dominate the individual and prove himself right by saying, "Yes, but I happen to know. . . ."

Neither duplicity nor blind impulsiveness is consistent with the Christian emphasis upon boldness. Boldness is not impulsiveness. And the opposite of boldness is not secret counsel. Paul makes this clear when he writes: "We have renounced disgraceful, underhanded ways; we refuse to practice cunning or to tamper with God's word, but by the open statement of the truth we would commend ourselves to every man's conscience in the sight of God" (II Cor. 4:2).

Boldness is the expression of a disciple who desires reconciliation. It must be in a spirit of personal powerlessness. Secret security is to be rejected.

Some Open Declarations

A transparent self is essential to a Christian witness. The minister must know himself. If he is to have a "tender heart and a humble mind," he will need some controlling attitudes. What are some that will enable a sympathetic servant to "speak the word of God with boldness"?

(1) Pastoral boldness rests upon an open admission of controlling principles. The Roman Catholic parishioner is assured of the seal of confessional. The Lutheran can look to the catechism, the Presbyterian to the Book of Church Order, the Methodist to the Discipline as the boundaries within which the minister will be bold. Within these areas of concern there are statements of principle, declarations of purpose.

For Baptists and Disciples the conversion experience and reliance upon the Bible are basic. I marvel at the inquiries that people in the South will admit from ministers. But they assume that the minister is concerned for their salvation or spiritual growth. So long as the pastor seems to have a primary concern for the work of the Spirit, he is accepted. When this is lacking, he is accused of "analyzing people" and meets resistance.

Southern Baptists have used the Bible so often to pound through their points with people that some students in clinical pastoral training want to disregard the Bible in counseling. I think they are wise to reject proof texts as a means of manipulation, but they are unwise to separate themselves from a biblical tradition. Guiding principles and applications from the Scripture are necessary both for the identification of the pastor before his people and as a source of appeal from the pastor to the congregation if the counselee feels that he is mishandled or misjudged.

Within the tradition of catechism or discipline, conversion, and biblical witness, the minister exercises freedom of speech. Those who seek his counsel may assume that he will be bold within these limits. This does not mean that everyone who sees the pastor will accept his presuppositions, but it does mean that they know what to expect from him. So long as he is accepted in this way, he is at liberty to inquire and respond. When a person does not accept him or his tradition, "boldness" would be foolhardy. (The minister is to be honest in either case, but to those who reject him the problem of witness and proclamation is to find some point of contact, some area of need where an unregenerate individual will admit his need of help offered in the spirit of Christ. In this chapter we are dealing with those who admit enough need to seek out a pastor for whatever help he offers within the tradition of his church.)

(2) A second controlling attitude is the minister's belief that he is a channel of God's grace among men and that the incarnation of God's grace in his attitudes and actions will help others to find strength and healing through God whom he serves. There is to be active godly power at the center of the pastor's ministry to men.

I find this belief badly shaken among ministers who are drawn to pastoral counseling. They sometimes identify with the occasional teacher or supervisor who says, "I can't think of anything we do that a psychiatrist doesn't do better."

The psychiatrist "does better" than such a teacher

because he believes that his method of healing is effica-cious.[3] It is no wonder that some ministers are timid when they doubt the benefits of Christian faith for personal growth. Without the impelling power of inner conviction, the pastor becomes a passive respondent to troubled people.

An uncertain pastor needs some assurance of power beyond himself to face problems such as the following: The mother of a young wife informed their pastor that her daughter and son-in-law were having difficulty. The daughter had just left her husband and two children for the fourth time. The pastor felt that he should call upon the husband, who was in obvious distress because he had to work and try to care for children at the same time. Yet the pastor knew that the man was not friendly to him and had never asked anyone in the church for help. When the pastor did call, he found the young husband to be hostile toward his wife and sure that he was right. Various reflective questions by the pastor led to this interchange:

HUSBAND: Let me ask you a question. How would you feel to go to work every morning with the fear of coming home to find your children and wife gone or to find the children alone without their mother?

PASTOR: I don't suppose I would like it.

HUSBAND: That's what I mean. I told her I would give her a divorce. She said this was agreeable to her.

PASTOR: (Arising) I would like to talk more with you

[3] Stein, *Contemporary Psychotherapies*, pp. 19-20.

later. I wanted you to know I am willing to do what I
can to help.

HUSBAND: I think I can handle everything.

The pastor went away assuring himself that it had been
a profitable call because the man had someone to talk
to. But on reflection he judged himself to have been too
sympathetic. He had not looked at the problem of
marital discord *with* the husband; he had only responded as the husband saw the problem. He had not helped
this confused and angry young man to evaluate his own
stability or his wife's maturity.

(3) A minister should proceed with caution, but he
should proceed. A third controlling attitude of pastoral
boldness is a willingness to test our conclusions and
judgments with the individual as we are forming them.
We have some power, but not the power of omni-
science. Therefore we must check our opinions with a
person at each stage of our relationship.

Our illustration of this need is the subjective judgment that follows nonverbal communication. A pastor
may notice that the person who has come to his office
is not looking at him. Instead, the individual shifts his
eyes from side to side, much as the pastor has observed
him doing in conversations with others in church. It
seems to the pastor that this manner betrays much un-
easiness, but the person speaks without hesitation. So
the minister asks:

PASTOR: I notice that as we talk you tend to look first at
one thing and then at another.

COUNSELEE: That is because I don't see you very well.

PASTOR: I don't understand.

COUNSELEE: Didn't you know? I guess it happened before you came here. I had an eye operation that allows me to read all right but leaves objects as far away as you in a blur. I know you are there all right, but I can't tell much about your expression.

Sometimes the open admission of our judgments is an affirmation of our like or dislike for an individual. We do not know if we should retain those impressions, and so we make them known.

So, for example, a pastor may hear of the ways in which a church leader has played up to other pastors and talked behind the backs of those who did not respond favorably to him. Hearing these rumors, one pastor told a leader who approached him for help:

PASTOR: I am glad to see you because I have heard something about you that I need to clarify. I hear that you are always talking to men in authority, that you flatter them to their faces but talk behind their backs if you do not agree with what they say. This I have heard, but not observed. It causes me to distrust you, and I doubt if I can help you much so long as I feel this way.

LEADER: Well, I do not know who would say that! It is true that I talk to my pastors because I think they are men of learning who can teach me a great deal, but I have always prided myself on telling a man exactly what I thought. I don't see how anybody could say that I criticize people behind their backs.

PASTOR: I don't know what the actual situations are. Give it some thought, and let me know if you can figure this out. If nothing comes to you right now, we can move ahead to discuss what you wish to and return to the problem of distrust at another time.

The leader later returned to say that he knew of some instances from two years before when he had expressed many anxieties about the opinions of former pastors. He explained that he felt very insecure at that time and had a bad habit of "blowing it out" to everybody. He felt that this problem was under better control and that he was taking more *responsibility* now for what he said. He also admitted that he now had some distrust of the pastor but was willing to take his time to make a final judgment, just as the pastor had given him a little time.

This desire to test our conclusions is in line with Paul's proclamation in II Corinthians 4. Although Paul's statement applies primarily to the preaching of the gospel, the spirit would be that an open statement of the truth is always better than "underhanded ways."

I am not advocating an impulsive statement of every opinion that comes to an untrained counselor. I am saying that a man who knows himself and others should humble himself enough to test his own judgment against those whom he has judged, whether his opinion is favorable or unfavorable.

(4) A fourth controlling attitude is the acknowledgment that we cannot change a person by our words or the power of our personality. That is, we cannot change

them in the Christian sense of conversion, transformation, or regeneration. We can be messengers, ambassadors, witnesses. We are not kings with power over the lives of others.

When we openly admit our strengths and limitations, then the power we do have as representatives of God can be controlled. I fear the hidden persuader, whether he be psychiatrist, marriage counselor, pastor, or advertising expert. But I notice that some pastors are unwilling to test their ideas openly. Secretly, they believe that their opinions would devastate another person. When I ask them if it has really happened, they tell of the great care with which they inhibit any verbal communication of their power. They have not tested themselves in the realities of interpersonal discussion.

Pastoral boldness means that a minister does "not think more highly of himself than he ought to think" because he has surrendered his strength to One greater than himself. One minister may admit to his counselee that there are times when he is domineering, attempting to order the lives of others. Another pastor may confess his tendency to keep silent because he is unsure of his judgments or anxious to keep goodwill. Such declarations would typify the New Testament usage of "boldness." It is the free utterance of God's love among men from those who were formerly shackled by fear or false pride.

(5) Finally, boldness is the belief that the godly quality of a relationship is more important than relationship for its own sake. If we are disturbed by the character of the individual, the deceptiveness of his

communication, we should show it in some way. We
want to make things clear so that the relationship can be
deepened or a person can be made better because of
what we say or do. In the process he may reject us, and
we should openly face this risk with him. We would
like to please persons and make circumstances easy, but
a power within us is always calling this into question.
We are to "admonish the idle, encourage the faint-
hearted, help the weak, be patient with them all" (I
Thess. 5:14). Our hope is to be for tranquility and
mutual edification, but the higher law of God's love
continually puts us and others to a test. The way in
which others receive the proclamation of love will determine the serenity or the severity of our relationship
to them (II Cor. 13:5-10).

The impelling power of truth is needed when a pastor
has community information about an individual. A pastor may not know if the individual is aware of the gossip
or the amount that has come to the pastor. For example,
a pastor heard that a young schoolteacher was dating a
divorced man. The young lady was quite interested in
the man, but no one knew how interested he was in her.
Occasionally he came to church but had little to say to
the pastor or anyone in the community. The pastor
thought that the man was aware of strong community
feelings against divorce. The young lady had talked to
the pastor about this problem: why does he continue
to pay attention to me but postpones any idea of
marriage?

One afternoon the pastor had gone by the school at
the teacher's invitation to discuss the theological and

community problem of "dating a divorced man." In the midst of their discussion her friend who was divorced came into the room. The pastor talked of his pleasure in seeing the man and how nice it was that he came by to take the young teacher home from the school. He did not mention any of the issues that were so openly discussed before the divorced man came in.

Later the pastor wondered why he was not able to "get close" to this man. Although the minister is by nature a "manly," open person, he felt that his community role required concealment. When we discussed the possibility of acting with authority despite criticism, he felt more assured of his ability to speak forthrightly to persons in the future.

Occasions for Pastoral Initiative

The virtue of pastoral boldness can be demonstrated only when the attitude of truth gives specific occasion for its proclamation. What are some of the times and places when it is called for?

First, pastoral boldness is required when a pastor has received information in the community that may be a source of strength or detriment to an individual. Two examples of this have been given. In one a pastor explained the way in which previous information conditioned his trust of a church leader. In the second a pastor knew that community feelings about divorce influenced all the relationships of which he was a part but refused to declare this openly to a divorced person.

The information that is passed on from the pastor

may be positive or negative. So long as the "good tidings" are communicated in a spirit of realism and with a knowledge of human limitations, they are a potential source of strength to an individual.

A second occasion for free speech comes when a pastor knows of a crisis that should be discussed with concerned persons. For example, a pastor visited a woman several days before she was to re-enter a hospital for her third operation. Her husband stayed in the room for a few minutes, and then he excused himself. The wife commented that her husband's stomach had been bothering him in the past few weeks. She said that he was becoming quite nervous.

On the following Sunday the pastor saw the husband at church and noted that his attitude was cold rather than cordial. A week later the husband, a church officer, came to the pastor's office to discuss an administrative decision. After this was clarified, the pastor talked of the condition of the man's wife and then asked how the man felt about his wife's condition. The husband said that he did not know if his wife would survive this operation. When the pastor asked about the husband's feeling concerning death, the husband said that he could hardly stand the thought of losing his wife. He did not know what to do. He was just now realizing how much he felt about her. The pastor asked if he had ever talked over things with his wife. The husband said "No," remained silent for a few seconds, and then said that he had to see about some Sunday school business.

On the following Sunday the pastor noted that the husband's attitude toward him was much improved. He told the pastor of the date when his wife was to have her operation and that he had arranged for a deacon who was to be with him at the hospital to call the pastor as soon as the surgery was over. He wanted the pastor to know of his wife's condition.

In evaluating these conversations, the pastor admitted that he had much anxiety about an open conversation with this powerful man in the church. But he felt that the husband was enduring much anguish without relief and that someone should help him openly to express his fear of death and his love for his wife.

Boldness is also required when a pastor knows of a practice or attitude in a friend or counselee that makes a difference in their relationship. Sometimes an open proclamation of our feelings may lead to counseling, or if it occurs during counseling, may deepen—or destroy —the relationship.

A wife consulted her pastor on several occasions about marital difficulties which included her reaction to her husband's heavy drinking. She felt that her husband would not talk to anyone about his drinking problem, even though he enjoyed the sports of hunting and fishing with the pastor. Presently, the wife telephoned the pastor to say that she was under so much tension that she was ready to begin divorce proceedings. She wanted to know if the pastor would talk with her husband.

When he called on the husband, the pastor said that the wife had mentioned a divorce. The pastor indicated that he had known about these marital difficulties for some time and had encouraged the wife to ask her husband to come for pastoral counseling. He also said that he knew of the heavy drinking of the husband.

PASTOR: Did you know that I knew of these things?
HUSBAND: No.
PASTOR: Does it make any difference in our friendship?

Again the answer was no. The husband then said that he wanted to work out things if it were not too late. For an hour and a half the two men talked.

The wife was surprised and relieved to hear from the pastor that her husband had talked so freely about marital problems. Soon after this, the husband called and asked the pastor to go hunting with him. As they walked along together, the husband began to talk about his drinking and to say that for the first time he was willing to admit that it had the best of him. He could see it in the way that it had wrecked his marriage.

Another occasion for boldness comes when an individual seems to be deceiving himself deliberately and asking that the pastor accept this deception. One eighteen-year-old boy came to his pastor to say that he needed some help in getting along with his parents. He felt rejected at home. During the time between several interviews the pastor learned that the boy was doing very poorly at school and had said that he would drop out before he graduated. When the pastor mentioned this to the boy in their subsequent interview, the boy replied that this was what he was really so anxious about in relation to his parents. They did not know that he was doing so poorly in school. He wanted to join the

Army and make it appear that this was his reason for dropping out of school. When he asked the pastor if this were not the best way to solve the problem, the pastor disagreed. He said that a high school diploma was very valuable and that the boy was refusing to face his own lack of motivation. Deceiving other people would not help.

The boy left school a month later and joined the Army. After a year he returned on leave and came to see his pastor. He said that he was looking for a transfer to another base because things were not going well for him at the base where he was stationed. He placed the blame for this upon many persons in authority. The pastor said that this sounded exactly like the conversation of last year when he placed blame on teachers and wanted to leave home. Now he wanted to leave one base for another. The pastor concluded, "I am willing to help where I can, and you know that I do care about you. I have written to you, and I have been ready to talk to you whenever you were here, but I do not think we are getting anywhere on your problems by acting as though they are nonexistent. Right?" The young man answered that he was glad to have somebody to listen to him and that he felt that the pastor did care about him. But he made no change in his plans and soon was transferred to another base.

There are some occasions when pastoral boldness may literally be the proclamation of good news. For example, a pastor may sense a change for the good (or for the bad) in an individual and make this known to him, before the individual has consciously sensed it. Or the pastor may think of something that would be helpful in solving a problem and present this to the counselee during their next interview.

One of these opportunities appeared on the second interview of a pastor with one of his Sunday school teachers. The teacher felt that she was not getting much respect or attention from the students. She wondered if she were adequate in the preparation of her lesson and her teaching techniques. During a discussion of her relationships with the students and an examination of her teaching method, the pastor found little to question. On the surface all seemed to be going well; yet he could sense her basic frustration in the class.

In the second interview the pastor said that he had been thinking about their conversation during the past week. He remembered that she had spoken very highly of a Sunday school class that she taught in another church "before my husband passed away." She had also talked of her loneliness after her husband's death. Was it possible that this new class, made up of girls in their teens, had become something more than just a class for her?

PASTOR: You have felt very alone without your husband?

COUNSELEE: Very much.

PASTOR: Was he a source of strength for you when you had that other class?

COUNSELEE: Then I felt I had more to give.

PASTOR: Because he gave you confidence?

COUNSELEE: (Silence.)

PASTOR: Do you think that you may be conveying to the

CLASS unconsciously that you have nothing to give
(pause) while you are needing something from them
that they can't give, that is mature adult friendship?

COUNSELEE: I never thought of it that way. I remember I
did not want to leave the ladies' class to teach this
class. I only took it because they almost shoved it on
me. (Pause) I guess I have lost contact with the ladies
that I enjoyed being with. My neighbors are not those
who share my interests.

PASTOR: Have you thought that there are times when the
church needs to serve its servants? You have been very
faithful as a teacher, but I am wondering if we should
not be faithful to you by moving you back to your
own Sunday school age group for a time?

COUNSELEE: I would love that.

PASTOR: We are not taking you out of service, because
you can add your part to the class discussion and help
the other members grow even as they help you by
general sharing of common interest.

COUNSELEE: Yes, at the other church I was helped so
much at Bob's death by those people. I learned to
deal with myself.

The widow then began to tell how she had learned to
recognize some of her own feelings of inadequacy. She
said that she had always felt quite dependent and looked
to the church as a place where people would give her
reassurance.

Leaning on Love

Penetrating conversations, like the second interview
with the widow, can be frightening to a pastor. Did he

go too far? Has he said too much? It is difficult to know
how to judge how bold we should be.

Then there are more shaking questions about self-
esteem. Have we exposed our own inadequacies, our
fears, and our prejudices? Have we misjudged a situation
and lost face by failure to keep contact? Have we been
rejected?

There is no reassurance that an aggressive servant of
the Lord will always do the right thing or that he will
be well received. Many times he will do or say the wrong
thing because he does not really size up the problem or
know himself at the time. Boldness is risky business.

So why take risks? Well, we cannot ask others to be
something we will not be. If we require "authenticity"
in others, how about it in ourselves? And others see us
as we are, so why pretend to hide? Either our honest
concern or our cunning bid for power will be manifest.

We really cannot call others to the love of God unless
we demonstrate some trust in him ourselves. One way
to show our trust in God is to expose our concern for
other people. They can accept or reject us. But we continue to remain vulnerable because their relationship to
God is more important than their good feelings about
us. For, as has already been stated, we are continually
seeking to lead men to something beyond ourselves, to
the ultimate source of all authority.

It really should not matter too much that a person
rejects a pastor. That could be a "personal" matter.
(The "personal" might need correction. Suppose the
minister were one of the immature students we met in
the previous chapter?) Most denominations have recog-

nized this limitation for ministers and have given members a fair chance to challenge such an authority, to talk back when they think he has gone too far. This is expressed in rules for church discipline, which usually say that a member cannot be admonished by a minister alone. Disciplinary action is a corporate function. The church, or a committee, must hear both sides and then give judgment. Thus both minister and member will have someone to lean on besides themselves. They can submit themselves to a fellowship of concerned Christians. The next chapter will show how this can be done.

7
Church Discipline

Church discipline is a court of appeal for both pastor and people. If the pastor needs to be sustained or restrained, this is to be done by the church in counsel or by an official board which carries this responsibility. The personal relationship that carries pastoral authority can be reinforced and broadened into group consensus, or the subjective distortions of the pastor's position can be modified or challenged by others who share basic Christian convictions.

Church discipline is a corporate form of care and supervision. As Chapter 2 has emphasized, responsibility for members was exercised by members in the early church. The Reformers grasped this truth again in their doctrine of the priesthood of believers. The present emphasis upon church renewal is based upon the responsibility for members of a group to care for one another and to reinforce one another in their care for the community.

This responsibility can involve some negative judgments. In the course of examining a problem, the church may find that the source of difficulty is a sick

111

and/or sinful person, or the distorted relationships that permeate the church from such sources. Then the congregation must go beyond sentimentality to censure. But to do this is to violate the modern stereotype of pastoral authority. Laymen do not think of "spiritual" advice in terms of judgment on a person's sin or exhortations to repentance (so far as we could tell from the survey reported in Chapter 4).

Yet some way must be found to restore the spiritual health of a congregation. When this issue is raised in pastoral or denominational conferences, there is general agreement that "something must be done," but the inevitable question is: How is it to be done? I have collected a number of successful and unsuccessful attempts at church discipline to obtain some clues about the corporate exercise of spiritual authority. There are not enough of these to draw any general conclusions at the present time, but I will present a representative story which usually gets the response: "Oh, I had an example just like that in my early ministry." Although the exercise of corporate discipline is necessary throughout a pastor's ministry, I have chosen a composite example from the early life of several ministers which will demonstrate the pastor's feelings, the struggles of members of the congregation, and the behavior of the people toward whom authority was directed.

The Head Deacon

The center of all conversation in Midland was the March business meeting of the village's church. At that time a committee of the church recommended that Deacon Riggs and Mrs. Riggs be suspended from membership until they ceased to disrupt the fellowship of the church. A change of action and attitude would be required as guarantees of their repentance. The motion had passed unanimously.

People understood why the church took such action against the man who called himself the "head deacon." Almost everyone could repeat some story of his own or a neighbor's run-in with Mr. or Mrs. Riggs. In the week after the business meeting the pent-up hostilities of years broke loose in continuous comments. It seemed as though the community now felt safe to air accumulated resentments against the former leaders of the church. One phrase was heard again and again: "They should have been disciplined years ago."

The Riggses brought a reputation with them when they moved into Midland. For years their family had owned land in a neighboring county and had "run" the county seat church. Several of Mrs. Riggs's relatives were ministers. One was an evangelist who liked to see a congregation "stirred up."

Feelings were soon stirred up in Midland. The Riggses wanted what they wanted "now!" Sometimes a store didn't have the goods they desired. One day, after Mr. Riggs had stormed out of the drygoods store, storekeeper Thomas said: "I've never seen a man get so mad because I couldn't sell him exactly what he wanted. He treated me like I was his mule."

Mrs. Riggs earned her reputation with the high school teachers. None of her children was exceptionally bright;

Mrs. Riggs blamed their low grades and occasional behavior problems on teachers, principals, and other students. "She'll call you on the phone in the evening and
just cut you down," said one teacher. Looking at the
children, folks decided that Mr. Riggs ruled with an
iron hand at home and expected to have instant obedience in the community as well. His children were never
known to talk back or contradict him in anything.

The Riggses' hostile ways did not prevent them from
being accepted into the Midland Church. In fact, some
people seemed to welcome a man who would "stand up
and say what he thought." Men did not say much in
the church. They seemed indifferent and indecisive. So
there was much good feeling when Mr. Riggs joined
the church and let it be known that he was an ordained
deacon who could "set some things straight" if he were
elected to serve in his new church home. No one asked
the members of his former church why he was moving
his membership. It seemed so natural, since he was now
living in town. He told people that he liked to be near
the mill in which he was a semiskilled worker.

In 1940 Mr. Riggs was elected deacon. He began to
tell church members that the deacons should make all
the real decisions for them: "Leave these matters to the
spiritual leaders; we know best." When the deacons
would meet, Mr. Riggs would be quick to make suggestions and volunteer his services. One deacon, Mr.
West, objected occasionally to Mr. Riggs's arbitrary
ways. The other deacons were quiet.

In two years Mr. Riggs had proved himself such a
willing worker that he was elected church treasurer. This

seemed to be the best way to get a man to lead things, until various church members proposed that the church borrow $15,000 to finance the completion of Sunday school building construction and sanctuary redecoration. Mr. Riggs and his family thought that the church should "save money and not spend it on paint and things like that." When the membership voted for the building and redecoration, Mrs. Riggs introduced a motion that no contract should be let until the church had "cash in the bank to pay for all construction." The motion failed.

In the months that followed, the Riggs family would introduce their motion for "cash in the bank" and be defeated. When told by the leading businessman in the town that the church had already defeated their motion, Mr. or Mrs. Riggs would reply that "this is a matter of conscience, and we can't rest until the church does the right thing."

Finally, Mr. Riggs declared that if the church did not pass the "cash in the bank" motion, he would resign as treasurer. "My conscience won't allow me to spend money that the church doesn't have," he said. There was silence. No one else wanted to be treasurer. After a few moments his motion was passed.

Mrs. Riggs told the ladies in the Sunday school class of which she was a member that the businessman was jealous of her husband: "You know, my husband has done well despite his lack of a college education. I don't have one either. But we know how to stand up to those educated people who try to keep us from getting ahead." She never said this openly in the church. It was always whispered to someone in a class meeting or stated in a long telephone conversation.

Other things were said over the phone. Mrs. Riggs spread the word that her Sunday school teacher was against her. She often called the teacher to say, "I don't know why you go out of your way to offend me, but I want you to know that some of the things you said this morning I don't agree with. You shouldn't talk that way in the Lord's house." The teacher had difficulty in understanding just how she gave offense, but she always knew when she had. At times Mrs. Riggs gave such unmistakable signs as turning her head away from the teacher and staring out the window during an entire lesson.

The Frustrated Committee

By 1946 the arbitrary actions of Mr. Riggs as treasurer and the gossip of Mrs. Riggs on the telephone led the church to send a committee to see them. Two men and two women were on the committee. One woman's husband told a deacon: "Don't ever put my wife on another committee of any kind. After what she's endured from the Riggses, I'm surprised that she comes to church at all." The deacon knew what he meant. Mr. and Mrs. Riggs were systematically tearing down the reputation of the committee.

The committee never reported publicly the results of their conversation with the Riggses. When members asked why, the pastor would say, "I believe that we should work in love to help everyone. The Riggses have explained their side to the committee. They want to stay in the church and work as hard as ever. I really don't feel that we should do anything but forgive and work together for the Lord."

Although the committee report died in the pastor's office, there were two obvious results of this encounter. First, people noticed that it was more difficult to get men into the church. They never had seemed too interested, but now they would not even come to worship services. Second, Mr. Riggs gained full authority for major church decisions. When the pastor resigned in a few months, Mr. Riggs announced that as head deacon he would be chairman of the pulpit committee. Unopposed, he chose friends to serve on the committee with him, talked to candidates for the pulpit, and told them that he paid all the bills, including their salary. The church had seven pastors from 1946 to 1957. Some were men who worked near Midland during the week and preached on Sunday. Others were seminary students. None opposed Mr. Riggs directly. As one seminary student told the few men who opposed Mr. Riggs, "If you don't like a church, leave it. That's what I plan to do."

The student pastor's advice came after a major church split in 1957. At that time several church officers and a deacon proposed a rotating system of deacons and church officers. Mr. Riggs and one other deacon opposed it. At a business meeting the pastor sought to explain the reasons for such a change. Mr. Riggs shook his finger in the young man's face and yelled: "Listen to me! We don't need any young squirt from school to tell us what to do. I've been with this church long enough to know what it ought to have, and this idea is not good for it. We're going to keep things as they are around here." And he did, for Mr. Riggs took the precaution to bring all the children and grandchildren to important business meetings. They obeyed him here as at home. By a close vote the new measures were defeated.

The pastor resigned. Mr. West, the only deacon who openly opposed Mr. Riggs, pleaded with him to stay. He asked, "How can we ever break this man's power if we don't have a pastor who will lead us? The people will rally round someone in whom they have confidence. But what can we do when preachers quit?"

Three men who were church officers resigned when the pastor did. The businessman who had been a major source of financial support withdrew his membership and joined another church. By 1959 only three men came regularly to the worship services and business meetings. Boys refused to attend church after they graduated from the junior department. Children, a few young mothers, and several elderly women were the usual Sunday audience. The church was dying.

The New Pastor

Pastor Long was called to Midland Church in the summer of 1960. Mr. Riggs was sulking at the time and did not come to church until weeks after the new pastor arrived. Mr. West had reproved Mr. Riggs for his offensive language to the last pastor, and Mr. Riggs had vowed that he would never support a pastor that Mr. West approved. Mr. Riggs was on vacation when Mr. Long was first invited for a "trial sermon." Mr. West and many others approved him.

Pastor Long's encounter with Mr. Riggs came during a deacons' meeting in the fall. Mr. Riggs spoke vehemently about the "stories spread by another deacon about me." He glowered at Mr. West. Pastor Long commented that it might be well for some of the more active people to rest for a while, restore their good feelings, and allow some of the younger people to take some responsibility. Mr. Riggs and Mr. West were silent.

Two weeks later Pastor Long dropped by Mr. Riggs's house to ask if preparations were being made for Communion on Sunday morning. Mr. Riggs replied hotly that he wasn't going to do anything: "Since you told me to sit back, I'll just sit back. Ha! Now see what will happen to the church. The young people of this church won't do anything." "Oh?" replied Pastor Long. "What won't they do?" "Why," said Mr. Riggs, "they don't wash dishes after a church supper like I tell them to. And lots of other things. Let me tell you, they may give occasionally, but we give the real money for your salary. So if you run us off, you won't get but half salary."

The pastor explained that he wasn't trying to run off anybody, and he wanted everybody included in church work. The conversation ended with a pronouncement from Mr. Riggs: "I can't serve the Lord's Supper Sunday. I won't be there Sunday. There's bad feeling between us. The Bible says you drink damnation with that. That's what *my* Bible says [pointing to the King

James Version]. It's God's Word, not the words of man, like that new revision you seminary fellows carry."

Several months later a new crisis developed with the Riggses. Mrs. Riggs complained that she had to do all the piano playing for the church. She felt that no one would help her. The pastor suggested that a music committee be formed and that they find an assistant for Mrs. Riggs. When he paid a routine visit to the Riggs home, he found Mrs. Riggs whimpering in the living room.

MRS. RIGGS: I don't want anything to do with your plan. You're just trying to get me out as pianist.
PASTOR: This committee is to help you so you won't have to do all the work.
MRS. RIGGS: (Crying) No, no! You're just trying to get rid of me. You can do anything you want, but don't come to me when it doesn't work.
PASTOR: I'm sorry that you feel that way.

Later, a woman on the music committee asked Mrs. Riggs to serve as pianist. Mrs. Riggs replied: "I'll play for my Lord, but not with any committee!" When this was repeated in the committee report, the pastor suggested that the spirit of Mrs. Riggs was not right to work with a committee and that some other arrangements for a pianist should be made. On the following Sunday, Mrs. Riggs said, as she left the morning service: "Nobody is going to get me to quit, because I was elected to serve this entire year. After this year I'll be out of your way, and glad of it!" Two weeks later the church found a new pianist. She was a former member who rejoined the church with the coming of Pastor Long.

Within six months after Pastor Long's first sermon, Sunday school attendance was at a record high of ninety. Men and women were beginning to return to the worship services. Mr. West was able to find four grown men each Sunday morning to take up the offering, and it was a pleasure to count the growing receipts. But there was still a cloud of misunderstanding about the function of the deacons in the church. Were Mr. Riggs, Mr. West, and Mr. Appleton to make the major decisions for the congregation, or were they to recommend at a business meeting such action as the whole church should act upon? To initiate discussion of this problem, the pastor asked that all church officers meet with him to prepare some report on the function of deacons.

Pastor Long did not know that this displeased Mr. Riggs until he dropped by to ask about a new neighbor of the Riggses' who might be a prospect for Midland Church. Mr. and Mrs. Riggs both had questions for him:

MR. RIGGS: Just what is this committee to do? It's like a butcher knife in my side. I guess you want me out.

MRS. RIGGS: Why did you do this? Why do you want to get rid of my husband?

PASTOR: I'm not trying to get rid of anybody. This is a committee to find our way out of some confusion.

MR. RIGGS: Listen, Long, I've told you that when you want to know about the deacons, you ask me. I'll call the meetings. When I ask, they come.

PASTOR: Yes, but you told me when I first came here that you'd never call them together so long as I was pastor. That's not right.

MR. RIGGS: I've done well by this church. No one is as faithful as I am; you know that.

MRS. RIGGS: Yes, and you've been telling things about us to everyone. Bad things. You wouldn't feel right if I told you all they've told me. (Mrs. Riggs's voice shook as she said this. She takes tranquilizers regularly.)

PASTOR: I should like to know what these things are.

MRS. RIGGS: Oh, no, you wouldn't! Ohooo (crying).

PASTOR: Well, is there anything else you wanted to talk about?

MR. RIGGS: Yes, why don't you preach the Bible? You said in your last sermon that we all ought to have a college education. That's not the Bible!

PASTOR: Wait a minute. I was talking about the need of young people today to get all the education they can, for Christians of the coming generation are going to face questions about science and faith that this generation has not. I think my sermons are biblical.

MRS. RIGGS: Just tell us why you are trying to get people against us. I don't understand. I don't want to start any trouble with anyone. You told people you didn't want me to play the piano.

PASTOR: I said that if you wouldn't cooperate with a committee, then your spirit wasn't right for that work at that time.

MRS. RIGGS: (Rocking forward in her chair and gritting her teeth) Oh, that's a lie, a lie!

PASTOR: Well, you're the one who told me that you needed an assistant.

MRS. RIGGS: Oh, after all these years as pianist, and now

you come along and do this to me. The nominating
committee never could get anyone but me. What are
you trying to do to me?

PASTOR: I'm trying to get you to work with the whole
church as a team.

MR. RIGGS: Ha! You told us deacons to sit back and do
nothing.

PASTOR: You keep wanting to throw that back in my face,
even though I have explained to you what I meant by
it.

MR. RIGGS: There's nothing for me to do but resign. I
don't know what else to do when you come in here
and lie to us and get things all stirred up. (He looked
at his wife, who was now gasping "Yes, yes" in a
hysterical echo.) We never had problems like this till
you came here.

PASTOR: For some reason there have been six pastors of
the church in six years. That's not normal.

MRS. RIGGS: God hears what you're saying. He knows.
Lightning is going to strike you. Something terrible
is going to happen to you if you keep talking like this.
(Her voice was then lost in sobs.)

MR. RIGGS: I think you ought to pray about this. I would
get down on my knees and pray!

MRS. RIGGS: (Screaming) Why are you saying these things?
Lying and carrying on like this!

MR. RIGGS: You are a stumbling block to us!

PASTOR: (Rising) I don't think I have to stay here and be
cursed by you.

MR. RIGGS: Don't accuse me of cursing. That's one thing
I've never done. You can't make up that kind of
story on me.

PASTOR: I have to go now; I don't think I can help you while you're like this. Good-bye.

The Church Action

Pastor Long told all this conversation to the congregation that night. He had gone from the Riggs home to the church moderator's home for supper. There he said: "I just can't preach. I'm so shaken by what happened with the Riggses." He began to cry. The moderator leaned across the table and replied: "Why, our church has been praying for years that this would happen. If Mr. Riggs resigns, it'll be the greatest thing that has happened to us. You did right, preacher."

With this encouragement Pastor Long went to the evening service and told the dozen people who were there that he could not preach. Instead, he had to unburden himself, to call on them for support and guidance. For forty minutes he told all his experiences with Mr. and Mrs. Riggs. To close the service, pastor and people formed a circle for prayer. Some who had never prayed in public were heard to pray during that circle in which there was not a dry eye. The pastor left the church with people saying to him: "Stay with us; we need you"; "we knew it would come someday, but no man would stay with us before."

The next morning Pastor Long called on a denominational official and a seminary professor for advice. Both counseled a course of church discipline, which worked out in this way. The moderator of the church and Mr.

West agreed with the pastor that a discipline committee should call upon the Riggses. The church voted this on the following Sunday night at a special business meeting. The committee, composed of men who had again become active in the church, were to admonish the Riggses for disrupting the church fellowship and calling the preacher a liar.

When the three committeemen called upon the Riggses, harmony seemed to be established. Mr. Riggs agreed that there had been dissension in the church. He then asked the men if they had searched their own hearts. Were they not also guilty before God? What man could cast the first stone? Perhaps, insinuated Mr. Riggs, there was a person in the church who really wanted an honest and faithful deacon removed. If so, Mr. Riggs asserted that he would not stand in the way of church harmony; he would resign. Mrs. Riggs said "Yes" to her husband's statements and hoped that the committee would lead all members of the church to look at their own lives and see where they had sinned.

As the three men went out of the Riggs home to their cars, one said, "You know, I guess we're doing wrong. Maybe the fault is with us." They stood in the dark under a tree to talk. Suddenly a thought struck one: "Say, neither of them admitted one little mistake themselves! Do you guess they just forgot to do that? I'll go back in and see if we just missed that part."

The good intention shattered the men's illusions about Mr. and Mrs. Riggs. For when the Riggses were asked about their own sins, Mrs. Riggs told them,

"You're stumbling blocks in our way to serve God!" The men asked if the Riggses would present their side to a business meeting. Mr. Riggs replied that he had nothing more to say. Anything from him to the church would be in writing. The committee retreated, abashed and wiser. As they drove home, one man said: "When they refused to come before the church, I knew they were in the wrong."

At the next business meeting the committee stated that the pastor's report was correct. The men felt that the Riggses were implacable. In fact, the couple were now saying that the pastor had called them liars. A letter from the Riggses was read to the church. It repeated accusations against Pastor Long and called upon the church to examine their own hearts for sin.

The congregation voted unanimously to suspend Mr. and Mrs. Riggs from membership until they showed action of repentance.

The Elements of Faithfulness

There are elements in the story of Midland Church that correspond to some of the biblical, historical, and modern findings concerning Christian authority.

First, there were a few people like Mr. West who stood their ground against Mr. and Mrs. Riggs for years. Without them the church would have dissolved. These are the "pioneers of the faith" who exemplify the meaning of ministry. They are committed to something beyond themselves which gives them power to maintain attitudes and actions of Christian faith. There is no discipline without this remnant in a congregation.

Second, most of the pastors of Midland Church had been the friendly representatives of God which were revealed in the questionnaires on modern attitudes toward the ministry. They had neither traditional, charismatic, nor professional authority. Even when the situation was so desperate that people sought their help, the clergymen advised submission, quietness, retreat, or positive thoughts.

Third, Pastor Long was unable to survive an attack from the Riggses by himself. He suffered for his open declaration of the problem as he saw it, and it brought him almost to the breaking point. He needed the understanding fellowship of church leaders and the support of the congregation for a restoration of his confidence and ministry.

Fourth, pastor and people postponed judgment on the Riggses for so long that discipline could only be devastating. To go back a number of years, what would have happened if the pastor or church leaders had refused to allow Mr. and Mrs. Riggs to gain leadership in the congregation? Restraint of their ambitions would certainly have preserved some health in the church and might have led them to see that all was not well in their own lives.

But there were not enough key leaders to take the risk of authority at the same time. This brings us to a basic spiritual problem in discipline. What is a person willing to suffer for the sake of his faith? We raised the question in this chapter toward the leadership who should exercise authority. In the next chapter we will consider the answer of one who is subject to discipline, a member with whom the pastor or congregation has shared an appraisal.

8
The Personal Response

How is it that one person accepts responsibility for his actions and another projects guilt upon others? Why do some people behave like the Riggses when their authority is challenged? Who can explain the reasons behind repentance, rejection of guilt, or drifting with easy indifference?

Questions like this are being raised in psychological as well as theological circles. Dr. Hobart Mowrer, research professor of psychology at the University of Illinois, has emphasized acceptance of guilt and penance; Dr. Viktor Frankl of Vienna considers the central question of therapy to be: Can this patient begin to see what life demands of him, and can he contribute willingly of himself to others?

These are ways of emphasizing personal responsibility. In this chapter we will see how the personal response to the mediated authority of a pastor and, beyond him, the authority of God is conditioned by home, ways of thinking, conception of the self before God.

The Conception of Authority

To begin with, there is the long-term conditioning of parental figures. It is in childhood that our conception of authority is molded. Here is where the "hidden" response to the ministry begins.

Even before a person sees a pastor, he has an idea of him as reasonable or unreasonable just because he is an authority. "Authority" is a word that develops very early associations in our minds. Our parents taught us that social expectations were reasonable and predictable or unreasonable and capricious.

The emphasis of a considerate parent is upon the development of moral tasks at the time when the child is able to respond. There is praise and there is punishment, but it is a balance between the convenience of the parents and the growing abilities of a youngster. Usually at age four or five a child is able to take praise and blame into himself, to make the words of parents his own.

One father saw this when his son was trying to take a nap. The five-year-old would slip a leg off the bed, but as soon as his foot touched the floor he would say to himself, "Foot, get back up in the bed!" After five minutes of reciting the words he thought his father would have said, he turned over in the bed and went to sleep. He was developing trust and self-direction. It will be some time before he will know how to use praise and punishment appropriately toward himself, but the ingredients of mature authority are now within.

When the child moves out of the home into grammar

school, new authorities emerge. If teachers are as trustworthy and considerate as parents, then adults will be seen as valuable authorities who wish the good of all men.

Of course, there is also the world of other children. Rules for play and fighting must be worked out. Learning to "play right" is an exercise in mutual acceptance of authority. There is some give-and-take in this play, and this causes trouble to some children. Why? Because they were taught *absolute* obedience to a set of rules. Parents required it. So the child may resent this and throw all restraints away. He disrupts the game—and the classroom. Or he may be very rigid and insist that the rules must be played just as he learned them. If he is too passive to protest, he is very uncomfortable. "His conscience bothers him," we might say.

What kind of conscience is this? It is *authoritarian.* The child assumes that all rules are made once, forever, and must not be questioned. Only if a very powerful person tells him to change will he do anything differently. He certainly would not want to make any changes himself! And, to be safe, he always consults an authority about the application of rules. Then he is free of responsibility.

This is the hidden picture that some people bring to a pastoral interview. They sit and wait for a great authority to tell them the rules, define their role, praise or blame them for the application of infallible fiats. They do not feel responsible in themselves; their mission is to obey those who make the rules.

Fortunately, there are many other people who can accept some responsibility for their thoughts and actions. They have developed a *rational* conscience. As children they were encouraged to see when a parent's orders should be absolutely obeyed and when circumstances would modify them. For example, one eight-year-old was playing near the edge of a fishpond. Her mother was afraid she would get wet. The mother, busy talking to friends, waved her hand at the daughter and said: "Go over and sit on the park bench until I call you. I don't want you to get dirty before we leave this party." Several minutes later the mother found her daughter some distance from the bench, looking at a flower bed. When the mother became angry, the child replied: "But, Mama, I did not want to stay where you told me to go because the bench had a wet paint sign on it. I was *trying* to keep my dress clean, like you said." This was a rational conscience in action. The child determined what means were most appropriate to fulfill an authoritative command. Such a child also learns to make appropriate decisions with peers. He abides by the rules of the game because he feels better this way and is showing consideration for those who play with him.

The Golden Rule begins to be a reality about this time. Cooperation replaces parental constraint. The youngster judges his behavior toward others in the light of their behavior toward him.

In contrast, people who live under absolute authorities are insensitive to the needs of others. They do not know how to distinguish good rules from better ones or how to apply with sensitivity the rules they have learned by rote. Custom is equated with righteousness. If a minister does what is "fitting," he is obeyed. If he asks penetrating questions, he is considered to be dangerous. It makes authoritarian people uncomfortable to be asked to reflect on the reasons why they think as they do. Besides, they have not been trained to know how they should judge actions. And they certainly do not look into their own motivations. All that was settled years ago.

In the Middle Ages priests were puzzled by the "scrupulous" persons who came again and again to confess minor sins. Here were persons who wanted to be told just what to do. But then they did not have enough confidence to believe that their penance was acceptable. Their basic self-judgment had been destroyed.

Under the pounding preaching of repentance many persons on the American frontier began to show the same symptoms. They wept for nights at the mourner's bench or came forward for rededication at every revival. They waited for someone to tell them what to do, but when they did it, they still were miserable.

In the twentieth century some pastors have learned that an authoritarian conscience requires careful management. We cannot accept the person's estimate of a pastor as all powerful, all knowing. Though urged to be so in a thousand ways, the minister must be most "reflective" with these people. Through the pastor's faith they may come to have faith in their capacity to make rational, religious decisions.

The Open and Closed Mind

An authoritarian conscience produces a closed mind. Dr. Milton Rokeach has investigated this way of thinking in *The Open and Closed Mind*. Other studies have been made by psychologists like T. W. Adorno, *The Authoritarian Personality*,[1] and popular writers such as Eric Hoffer, *The True Believer*.[2]

In these studies there are definable characteristics of a closed, authoritarian way of thinking. For one thing, facts are rejected if they threaten a preconceived opinion. More and more evidence can be brought in, but it will all be rejected. The person with a closed mind "knows in his heart what is right." Nothing in the present, adult world gets close to the parental decrees of long ago. He sees the world as his parents saw it, and that is duty and loyalty.

Furthermore, the major opinions of a closed mind are isolated from one another. The dogmatic individual may have half a dozen beliefs and may be able to change any of them without disturbing the others. His mind is like a flower: the petals can be twisted and rearranged, but he is undisturbed as long as each idea holds to the central stem of absolute authority. Whatever the authority says to believe, he believes.

The closed mind views the world, both in general and at any particular moment, as very threatening. This threat might be related to early experiences that would produce chronic anxiety. Dr. Rokeach found that stu-

[1] (New York: Harper & Row, 1950).
[2] (New York: Harper & Row, 1951).

dents who scored low on a "dogmatism scale" said that they were able to see good and bad in fathers and mothers, were influenced by a number of persons outside the immediate family, and experienced few symptoms such as nightmares or nail-biting. But students with closed minds tended to glorify their parents, were influenced by only a few persons outside the family, and had more symptoms of anxiety.

Finally, the formal content of beliefs in a closed system rests upon absolutely authoritative people. It might be parent, pastor, teacher, President. Everyone else is accepted or rejected according to his agreement or disagreement with this absolute judge.

Now what can a pastor's reaction be to all this? Most of all, he can proclaim the distinction between the relative authority of men and the absolute authority of God.[3] The closed mind is fixed on an idol, some mortal or moral system that claims the worship due to God alone.

Second, a pastor can look for the distinction between dogmatic and stiff minds. A dogmatic mind accepts no new evidence, so movement toward new logic is futile. A stiff mind is slow to bend, but if contradictions are shown, the person may return in a week to say, "I've thought over what you said, and I'd like to discuss that further."

Third, the approach to a closed mind must center upon the assumption that the world is a dangerous

[3] See Richard R. Niebuhr's discerning study of this point in *Schleiermacher on Christ and Religion* (New York: Charles Scribner's Sons, 1964).

place. This is the world view of dogmatism. But, as the biblical evidence showed in Chapter 2, a Christian is being freed from fear of sin, hell, death.

Dogmatic persons are unable to accept this assurance unless they undergo the world view–changing experience usually called "conversion." It begins in the self-concept, and it comes from a power beyond ourselves.

Without conversion, the dogmatic person may accept our ideas about peripheral subjects, just as long as we act like an authority in our pronouncements. So, if we quote the Bible or state a denominational position, he may bow and retire. He respects authority! But he has not changed his inner attitude. So we must be prepared for a fourth approach, a willingness to settle for whatever the closed mind can conceive of in us. Perhaps by grace, judgment, patience, we may establish a less fearful relationship. But it must start where the closed mind sees us.

The Assimilation of Judgment

Pastors will see some changes on the surface of dogmatic persons, but only direct confrontation with God will bring them to true self-judgment and responsibility. If a person is more open-minded, the acceptance of responsibility is more possible, but it is certainly not immediate. Usually, people go through states of unacceptance-acceptance of God's judgment as it is mediated through pastoral interviews.

Dr. Lowell Colston described these stages as he saw them in persons who came for counseling to a church and to a counseling center.[4] These were steps in the assimilation of both human and divine judgment:

(1) opposition, feeling that judgment is external;

(2) inquiry into the way he judges others and they judge him;

(3) binding together of self-other judgments with personal feelings;

(4) discrimination of opinions about self and others;

(5) testing of these discriminating opinions in concrete situations;

(6) discourse, conversation of the self before God as judge with the definite possibility of acceptance by God;

(7) transformation of the self before God, with change discernible to others.

In his study of twenty-five counselees Dr. Colston concluded that real transformation, "rebirth," occurred in few people, and only after painstaking movement in the self through stages that have just been described.

The minister is an authority, but his is the authority of sharing. He sees *with* the counselee, he encourages progressively deeper self-insight, he seeks to prepare one for confrontation with God.

The dedicated process of such counseling was summarized by Dr. Seward Hiltner from one of Dr. Colston's case studies:

For example, one of his parishioners, at the start of her pastoral counseling, felt very negative about herself in nearly

---

[4] "The Function of Judgment in Pastoral Counseling" (Ph.D. dissertation, University of Chicago, 1961).

all realms of life, accepted her extraverted sister's negative judgment on her indecision, wondered if she were also all wrong in relation to God. A general aura of negative judgmentalism hung over her entire life. Yet none of these judgments was discriminating. Hence none of them was really assimilated. By the close of her counseling, she had learned a good deal about being discriminating in her judgments. On the one side, she stopped feeling guilty because she was unlike the extraverted sister. On the other side, she was able to judge herself negatively, and hence correctively, when she began to slide into a "Poor little me" mood. Colston's sequence of stages does not move away from making judgments, but toward increased capacity for making discriminating judgments on one's own initiative, checked with the environment.[5]

This is the goal of pastoral authority, to help a person accept and relate to the power of God redemptively. The goal of craftsmanship, the ability to see self and others, is reconciliation, the true sight of a child of God.

The Acceptance of Suffering

The successful conclusion of shared appraisal depends upon the servant motif in both pastor and counselee. On the one hand, the minister must be a "slave" of Christ, seek the fulfillment of life according to God's will for each person, rather than according to the desires or convenience of the clergyman. In humility he shares with others the judgment that comes upon all,

[5] Seward Hiltner, "Judgment and Appraisal in Pastoral Care," *Pastoral Psychology*, XVI (Demember, 1965), 46-47.

including himself. His authority is derived, mediated, as well as immediate and personal. All this is part of his acceptance of authority.

On the other hand, the counselee must become a servant, one who willingly accepts appropriate judgment from God, who sees self as it is before another person and does not turn away and forget what has been seen. This calls for humility, surrender, obedience to a higher power.

Inevitably the test of discipleship is willingness to suffer. The servant, whether minister or counselee, must endure the anxieties of self-revelation, the doubts of self-actualization, the pain of repentance.

Professor Melvin Kimble of Northwestern Lutheran Theological Seminary studied the acceptance of responsibility in suffering of forty-eight patients in a state mental hospital. He combined these clinical insights with a year of theoretical study with Dr. Viktor Frankl in Vienna to produce the following qualities that are crucial in a patient's recovery:[6]

(1) The patient must become aware of his own worth. If he cannot learn self-respect, he cannot accept responsibility.

(2) The patient must recognize the defiant power of his human spirit. The rebellious nature of man must be reckoned with. Excuses about bodily complaints or problems in the hospital must be laid aside, and the patient must admit that the basic struggle is with his *self*.

[6] "The Acceptance of Responsibility in Suffering" (Th.M. thesis, Southern Baptist Theological Seminary, 1961).

(3) The patient must hope that there is some possibility of growth in this struggle with the self. That is, he does have some freedom, and he can exercise it for health and holiness.

(4) The patient must become aware of the eternal dimensions of human existence. There must be some search for an *ultimate* meaning of life, an explanation of suffering that goes beyond self toward God. This is the antidote for passive, irresponsible resignation.

(5) There must be a struggle for faith. The patient must risk the pain and uncertainty of moving from a static religion, or none at all, toward spiritual growth. He must be guided by realism, hope, and the promise of renewal. Out of this comes the refreshing reward of moral decision and personal respect.

The Restraints of Reconciliation

The studies of Kimble and Colston give hope that people can respond to godly authority redemptively. But neither these sources nor Rokeach or Adorno or Mowrer provides definitive answers to the question: How and why did this individual respond as he did to religious leaders or spiritual crises?

We stand under the restraint of inadequate information and power. The power of reconciliation is with God alone; his servants testify to what can happen; they cannot bring transformation to pass. What we can do is point beyond our own authority, our own adequacy, by life and words that portray our love for the image of Christ formed in us.

Index of Names

Index of Subjects

143